CW00538501

The Undoing of Polly Button

The Undoing of
POLLY
BUTTON

*The Tragic Life
and Bloody Murder
of Mary Green*

STEPHEN MOORE

Matador
9 Priory Business Park,
Wistow Road, Kibworth Beauchamp,
Leicestershire, LE8 0RX
Tel: 0116 279 2299
Email: books@troubador.co.uk
Web: www.troubador.co.uk/matador
Twitter: @matadorbooks

ISBN 978 1789018 837

British Library Cataloguing in Publication Data.
A catalogue record for this book is available from the British Library.

Printed and bound by CPI Group (UK) Ltd, Croydon, CR0 4YY
Typeset in 11pt Adobe Garamond Pro by Troubador Publishing Ltd, Leicester, UK

Matador is an imprint of Troubador Publishing Ltd

FSC
www.fsc.org

MIX
Paper from
responsible sources
FSC® C013604

For Tina

CONTENTS

A Note on Currency[1]

Pounds, shillings and pence were the divisions of the pre-decimal currency in the British Isles. One shilling is made up of twelve pence; one pound of twenty shillings, i.e. 240 pence. Pounds are represented by the £ symbol, shillings as 's', and pence as 'd'. 'Three pounds, two shillings and one penny' is written as £3 2s 1d. 'Two shillings and six pence', referred to in speech as 'two and six', is written as 2s 6d, or 2/6.

The story of Polly Button is one significantly influenced by periodic and at times severe depressions affecting the local ribbon weaving community. Demonstrating the scale and extent of such adversity and financial collapse through the use of comparative or relative values (for example by converting nineteenth-century prices into contemporary ones) can be difficult, if not futile. Much depends on the context of the comparators chosen to make the comparison. However, two websites are recommended as being useful in understanding comparative values. First, a general introduction and links to other resources on this complex subject is provided by: http://projects.exeter.ac.uk/RDavies/arian/current/howmuch.html. An online calculator for assessing comparative values in a variety of ways is given at https://www.measuringworth.com/index.php.

A Note on Footnotes

Footnotes provide specific references to relevant source documents and websites and are given in order to provide evidential confirmation of the associated details contained in the text. Readers' enjoyment of the story will not be diminished should such footnotes and references be considered after finishing the book.

---

1   Flanders, J. (2012)

Johnny Danks, he played his pranks
Upon poor Polly Button.
He drew his knife, to please his wife,
And cut her up like mutton.

(*Local children's skipping rhyme*)

THIS HARD LAND

An Introduction to the Undoing of Polly Button

Mary Green, who went by the nickname Polly Button, was murdered by John Danks on the evening of Saturday, 18 February 1832. But she was not the first Mary Green thought to have been murdered in Nuneaton. That dubious honour belongs to a Mary Green believed murdered by her husband, Edward, in 1788.[2] The 44 years that separated the two deaths saw the once healthy silk ribbon weaving industry that dominated the town end in a period of steep decline, with the deep depression in the winter of 1831–2 marking the start of perhaps the worst ever year in Nuneaton's history. Nuneaton's *annus horribilis* began with Polly Button's murder, was followed by the outbreak of cholera in the town for the first time in the autumn and ended with the General Election riot on 21 December 1832. Perhaps because of the brutal and bloody nature of Polly Button's death, born out of the poverty and despair of the period, her murder remains possibly the most notorious in the town's history. The story has persisted over the last couple of hundred years through the oral tradition, occasional newspaper articles and publications, the performances of at least three plays and, last but not least, a rather grisly and memorable skipping rhyme.

---

2   Archenholtz, p. 288.

Fig. 1. Polly Button's house, 8 Friary Street, Nuneaton c. 1937 (side view, from Friary Street, looking eastwards).

Polly Button's notable nickname perhaps provides one reason for the story's persistence. Polly is a derivative rhyming nickname for Molly, itself used as a nickname for Mary. It has been widely suggested that the 'Button' element of her nickname arose because of her fine skills in button-working. Cyril Marden, the author of the first book on the murder of Polly Button, recalled an interview he had held with a lifelong resident of Abbey End, who retold a story of a shawl allegedly made by Polly Button being passed down through several generations of a family. The description of the shawl was that it was beautifully worked over the shoulders and cape, with many small black buttons of various shapes that produced numerous pretty patterns.[3] Although this story seems to support the origin of her nickname being derived from her close work with buttons, no documentary evidence has been found to confirm this. However, an additional explanation might be offered by the fact that her nephew, James Green, was known by the nickname Billy Button,[4] leading to the possibility that the surname 'Button' could have been used as a local nickname for this branch of the Green family in Nuneaton.

The events of that wintry night must have been the talk of the town for weeks afterwards, as the gruesome details of the murder were revealed – initially as gossip, then outlined at the inquest held a few days later at The Britannia public house, one of the town's many inns, and then detailed in full at Danks's trial at the spring assizes at Warwick Crown Court in late March. There are scant physical reminders left in the town. No gravestones exist for either

---

3   Marden, p. 7.
4   *Leamington Spa Courier*, 6 Aug 1831, p. 3.

of the two main people involved. Polly Button was buried in a pauper's grave at St Nicolas Church, Nuneaton, while Danks's body was taken down from the gallows and transported to Birmingham Medical School for dissection. The house in which Polly Button had lived was demolished in October 1940[5] (known at that time as 8 Friary Street). Fortunately, a photograph had been published just three years earlier in an article about the murder of Polly Button in the *Midland Counties Tribune* on 5 March 1937. The faded photograph in that article is the only image of Polly Button's house known to exist, a digital image of which has been taken and enhanced for reproduction in this publication (see Figure 1).

The barn where Danks attacked Polly Button after luring her from her home with an invitation to go out for a walk has similarly been demolished, although an image of the ruined remains of the building was also published in the same 1937 *Midland Counties Tribune* article about the murder (Figure 2).

The only physical object known to exist with a definite link to Polly Button's story is 'The Polly Button Stone' – a block of stone measuring 81 x 44 x 31cm that contains a carving of two effigies that had, at some point in the past, been set high into the wall near an entrance into Polly Button's house. Figure 3 is an illustration featured in Cyril Marden's book, *The Murder of Polly Button*, that shows the position of the stone in the façade of the front of the house.

Marden reported that during the demolition of the building, the foreman of the demolition gang had arranged for the stone bearing the

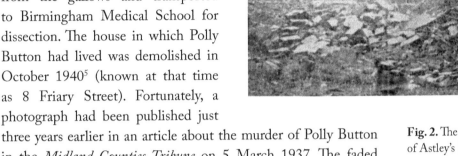

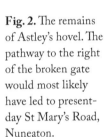

Fig. 2. The remains of Astley's hovel. The pathway to the right of the broken gate would most likely have led to present-day St Mary's Road, Nuneaton.

Fig. 3. Polly Button's house (facing south, from Friary Street). Illustration from Marden's *The Murder of Polly Button*.

---

5   Marden, p. 46.

Fig. 4. The Polly Button Stone as found in storage at Nuneaton Borough Council's St Mary's Road depot, 1970s.

effigies to be removed for safe keeping to the Nuneaton Borough Council depot just a few hundred yards away in St Mary's Road. There the stone remained until A. E. Jebbett, the editor of the *Midland Counties Tribune*, received a letter in 1955 informing him of the presence of the stone in the council yard. Jebbett sought out the stone and had it photographed for an article in the newspaper on 6 May 1955 entitled '*The Tragedy of Jack Danks and Polly Button, A Passionate Love Story Ended in Murder*'.[6] The stone then again seems to have slipped into obscurity and could have been lost for ever had Marden not started making enquiries about it in the early 1970s.

After interviews with council officials, he was given permission to search the council yard. Marden found the stone, still intact, lying amongst a pile of reclaimed bricks and some old-fashioned kerb stones (Figure 4). Marden was instrumental in getting the stone safely removed to the Nuneaton Museum & Art Gallery in Riversley Park, Nuneaton, where it now forms part of the town's Local History gallery (Figure 5).[7]

The stone had probably graced one of the much older buildings in the locality. It had been thought that with the recycling of building materials being quite common practice, the stone had been incorporated into the fabric of Polly Button's house at some stage in the past. One report, quoting a local resident, suggested that the stone figures had been set into the wall by the father of a Mrs Jeffries, one-time owner of the property.[8] Given the date of this report, it would seem that the insertion of the stone had been done after the murder of Polly Button, most likely in the mid-

6   Jebbett, p. 6.
7   Marden, pp. 45–6.
8   *Nuneaton Evening Tribune*, 4th December 1970, p. 14.

Fig. 5. The Polly Button Stone, Nuneaton Museum and Art Gallery.

to late-nineteenth century. Perhaps not surprisingly, a local myth sprang up that the stone showed the heads of Mary Green and John Danks. Marden recalled locals being attracted by the folklore of the stone effigies and peering through the windows of the house in curiosity.

It was this myth that triggered a recent approach to experts in such carvings to enquire if they might be able to shed any light on the origin or purpose of the stone effigies. One expert's view was that the stone carving was very unlikely to be medieval in origin due to its crude execution and the lack of any features or context that would link it to the Middle Ages. His opinion was that the stone may have been carved in the sixteenth or seventeenth century when stone carving was still relatively common. It could possibly have been taken from a house of that date that was being demolished.[9] Another source advised that houses and other secular buildings used to bear protective devices carved in stone or wood in a range of forms, including figures and faces. The carvings were thought to protect buildings and their occupants from evil entities. They

---

9   Email correspondence (19 August 2018) from Richard Halsey, MBE, architectural historian.

are known under the term of 'apotropaic', which means something which has the power to avert evil or bad luck. They have been found on or in medieval and later churches, and medieval and later stone and timber-framed halls, manor houses, farmhouses and cottages, as well as public houses, shops, and agricultural buildings. They are rarer on later and other types of buildings, although there are instances of similar devices being re-created on such buildings in a copycat fashion – as may have been the case with Polly Button's house. Each type of figure has a meaning, which in its symbolism protects the occupants of the house from evil influences and, like churches, they often appear near entrances or openings.[10] The fact that the stone was not used as a load-bearing lintel at Polly Button's house and was positioned near the doorway would appear to reinforce the view that the carved effigies had been deliberately placed there for apotropaic reasons and that this was done at some point after the murder to ward off evil. A reasoned assumption can subsequently be made that the turning away of evil in this instance was that linked specifically to the murder of Polly Button by John Danks.

However, the paucity of physical links hasn't stopped the story being perpetuated over the years owing to the bloody and awful circumstances of the murder. One local resident vividly recalled his mother observing the warning from previous generations 'not to go down the Burgage'.[11] My awareness first came in the oral tradition of the story being continued through Polly Button's descendants, of which my wife is one. She remembers clearly throughout her early years her mother pointing out the place where their ancestor had lived. In addition to the occasional newspaper article (e.g. *Midland Counties Tribune*, 5 March 1937, and *Nuneaton Evening Tribune*, 4 December 1970) the story has been retold, in varying degrees of accuracy, in several publications and websites, for example:

- *The Murder of Polly Button* (Cyril John Marden, 1977) – the most comprehensive account so far.

---

10   Fairey (2008)
11   Letter from Anthony Cole, *Nuneaton Evening Tribune*, 18 February 1964, p. 2.

- *Warwickshire Murders* (Chapter 1 – Poor Polly Button) (Betty Smith, 1991)
- *Warwickshire Murders* (Chapter 1 – A Deadly Secret) (Kevin Turton, 2007)
- *In and Around Haunted Nuneaton (Ill-Fated Polly Button)* (Jonathon Moss, 2011)
- *The Murder of Polly Button by John Danks* (http://www. weddingtoncastle.co.uk/polly-button.html)

Marden's book is an impressive piece of research and detective work, the product of dogged, detailed and, in those pre-internet days, a very time-consuming examination of parish registers and local newspaper accounts. Marden's interest in Polly Button was similarly prompted by his wife, as when they began courting she and her family lived in the house that had been the dwelling of Polly Button all those years ago. Marden described the building as follows:

> *The cottage had very low ceilings…with plenty of dark brown woodwork about on stairs, doors, window frames and cupboards. The coal-place was under the stairs and opposite the pantry. Ceilings were white-washed, and the floors red-tiled, not forgetting the brindle-coloured bricks the house was built with, and the blue small paving stones around the yard. There were two doors, one being at the side of the house [elsewhere described as the front] over which the effigies were placed, and the other door at the back, which at one time led out to the Twitchell Yard and Abbey Street. The cottage stood facing Friary Street, with its access leading onto this street. It was a three-storey house, the top floor being the work-room which was used during the time when ribbon weaving was then the major industry of the town. The blue-tiled pathway which led round the cottage was the access from the house into Friary Street, but in early times, before the street was in existence, the front of the house looked out upon open fields and across the Burgage Walk. It was here, backing onto the fields, that the privy was situated, and the blue-tiled path ran in that direction.[12]*

---

12   Marden, p. 45.

Fig. 6. Promotional poster and admission ticket for Pranks, 1982.

Despite there being limited physical references available to us as we try to picture the environment in which Polly Button lived and died, there are many other sources of information that can provide us with significant and clear insight into the circumstances and events that shaped Polly's tragic life, and directly contributed to her death when just 39 years old. For example, a play, *The Ghost Walk of Weddington*, was written and performed in local theatres within two years of her death.[13] This play was the only one written about the murder of Polly Button until Gef White, company and stage manager at the Belgrade Theatre, Coventry, and ex-journalist, wrote, produced and directed the play *Pranks*, performed by the Milby Theatre Society between 27 April and 1 May 1982 at the Nuneaton Arts Centre in Pool Bank Street, Nuneaton (Figure 6). The play was a period comedy set in Nuneaton a couple of years after the murder. Its cast included Joe Haddon, the parish constable who had arrested Danks and had given extensive evidence at both the inquest and subsequent murder trial. *Pranks* was written and performed in commemoration of the 150th anniversary of the murder.

It would also appear that the story was chosen by one local school (Manor Park) for their entry in a regional playwriting competition in the mid-1980s. The school's entry, a half-hour play written in rhyme and covering the circumstances of Polly's murder by John Danks, was performed at Warwick Arts Centre.[14]

Newspaper accounts from 1832 contain reports on the circumstances of the case, the evidence given at the coroner's inquest in Nuneaton that followed shortly afterwards, and full details of the court proceedings that took place just over a month later at the assizes in Warwick. It is, however, *The Ghost Walk of*

13   British Library Playbills 271. The playbill references a performance on 26 December 1833 at Atherstone Theatre.

14   Comment to author by Neal Evans, ex-Manor Park School pupil (25 July 2017).

Weddington that gives us an opportunity to understand something of the dramatic undercurrents that were to sweep Polly Button away to her death. Intended as sensational melodrama but containing elements of social realism, the play opens with the murdered body of Polly Button being revealed on a darkened back-lit stage and proceeds to tell of the circumstances that led up to her murder. The town's weavers are depicted grumbling about the power looms that have created mass unemployment in the ribbon weaving trade that dominated the town. This led to a daily struggle to deal with the poverty and destitution that had arisen, despite the efforts of the overseers of the poor in trying to hold society together in those desperate times. Personal animosity was known to exist between Polly Button and Danks's wife, Jane, with reports of arguments and open hostility well known in the neighbourhood. The play provides perhaps the most contemporary, compelling and insightful account of the forces that drove Danks to commit murder.

As research into the story of Polly Button progressed it became apparent that any definitive account of her life and murder would need to cover more than just the couple's background, Danks's vicious attack, and the trial. Two significant additional aspects were found to lie at the heart of a unique and desperately sad story.

First, the fundamental and critical impact that silk ribbon weaving had on the lives of most people living in Nuneaton in the late eighteenth century and early nineteenth century, and on Polly Button and Danks in particular leading up to 1832. This will be illustrated by reference to:

- The relevant aspects of the technology used, with Nuneaton proving unable or unwilling to adopt more advanced and productive looms.
- The organisation of the trade, which saw Nuneaton increasingly isolated and impoverished at the margin of silk ribbon production in the area.
- The move to free trade after 1826 that exposed the town to the icy blast of competition from cheaper, high quality ribbons, from France in particular.

The consequences for Nuneaton in the few years prior to 1832 were devastating. The depressions caused widespread poverty, hunger, ill-health, social unrest, suicides and bankruptcies. It is through an awareness of these societal ills that we can better understand the dire circumstances in which Polly Button struggled to find the means to live and raise a family.

Second, as more details about the fathers of Polly Button's five children were uncovered, it became apparent that the story was even more tragic than previously thought. After her first relationship, which had the potential to give Polly Button so much in life, her subsequent relationships would appear to have become increasingly born out of necessity or desperation (for love or money we will never know for sure). They all required action by the overseers of the poor to seek maintenance payments from the five men adjudged to be the fathers of her children. Even then, fate did not look kindly on Polly Button in these harsh years, as three of the five men so identified died relatively young and the payments from them under filiation (bastardy) orders would have stopped.

Inevitably, as research into the Polly Button story progressed, the question arose as to what had become of her five children after she was murdered. This telling of the story of Polly Button therefore includes an account of the fate of her children. In what is likely to be a unique element of research into Polly Button's story, efforts have been made to map out Polly Button's family tree and to trace as many of her descendants as possible through to the present-day. Consequently, a family tree comprising a total of almost 4,000 individuals has been established through genealogical research. Within this family tree in excess of 2,100 direct descendants have been identified, of which more than 1,000 have been confirmed as being living descendants. When approached with information about their connection to Polly Button, the enthusiastic response of descendants and their desire to know more about her story bears witness to an enduring fascination with what must surely constitute one of the most tragic and bloody murders in the country's history, born out of both economic and personal desperation.

So, let the story begin…

DEATH TO MY HOME TOWN

Nuneaton: The Scene of the Crime

Location and Some Relevant Local History

Nuneaton is England's most central town, located just five miles
from its geographical centre (52°33'42.9"N 1°27'53.5"W).[15] There
is some evidence from finds of pottery, kilns and coins locally that
the area may have been occupied in Roman times, an assumption
perhaps strengthened by the presence of Cambrian rock in the
Tuttle Hill range that might have been used to pave the Watling
Street Roman road that passed nearby. Nuneaton derives its name
from the Anglo-Saxon Ea-tun (farm by the water), the original farm
homestead developing over several centuries from an Anglo-Saxon
settlement into a post-Norman vill or township. The first written
reference to the township, as 'Etone', is in the Domesday Book of
1086, the survey made for William the Conqueror. This recorded
the presence of a mill, a use that continued on the same site on the
banks of the River Anker near the town centre until the demolition
of the last mill building on 31 March 1973. The settlement was

---

15 https://en.wikipedia.org/wiki/Centre_points_of_the_United_Kingdom,
   accessed 27 July 2017.

located on the eastern bank of the River Anker, where it lay in a deep river bend which served as a defensive barrier on three sides. In 1155, St Mary's Benedictine Priory was founded on the western side of the river, about one mile to the north west of the existing village and close to the Barpool brook that ran into the Anker. The priory's chief endowment was the manor (estate) that covered what became increasingly known as 'Nun-Eaton', Attleborough and parts of Stockingford. The priory needed to secure its long-term financial security and therefore proceeded to develop Nuneaton, beginning the change that would take it from a village to a town.[16]

One of the priory's first successes was obtaining a royal grant in 1160 for a weekly market, eventually settling on Saturdays some time later. The market had to be located on the western side of the river, as the eastern side was already fully taken up by the original village. The site eventually selected was on land owned by the priory at the junction of the roads to Coventry and Atherstone where, perhaps unsurprisingly, the present-day Market Place is located. The weekly market continues to this day and, indeed, took place on the Saturday that Polly Button was murdered. The town's subsequent growth was on this western side of the river, primarily following the road to Atherstone (now Abbey Street) between the Market Place and St Mary's Priory. Nuneaton's population grew in line with its economic importance to the area and began to attract traders and craftsmen into the town, transitioning from an agrarian economy to a broader one incorporating other trades and commerce. To attract newcomers, burgage plots were also offered by the priory through a charter of 1227. Burgage plots were divisions of the 'open' fields belonging to the manor that became enclosed, thereby extending the boundaries of the town. The burgesses to whom these plots were allotted, as tenants of the enclosed lands, paid a cash rent instead of giving feudal service as would have been required previously. The plots were long and narrow, measured approximately 15m x 45m and formed the basis of the ribbon development that took place along Abbey Street in the next phase of Nuneaton's growth. Over the years, many of the original burgage plots became sub-divided lengthways into half-burgages, with frontages of only about 7.5m, to

---

16   Veasey, Chapters 1 & 2.

allow for even more dwellings without extending the built-up area. The court containing Polly Button's house was to be built on one of these burgage plots. Concentrating the expanding population in dense developments created problems typical of urban growth, with concerns about the state of the town being recorded as early as the 1570s, sufficient for Manor Court regulations to be issued:

Fig. 7. Market Place, Nuneaton, c. 1890s.

> *A payne made than no person shall sweepe downe any muck in the stretes to th'annoyance of his neighbour but shall carye it away in payne of every defalte. 4d.[17]*

As Nuneaton slowly developed into a bustling town based around its market and an increasingly commercial centre, it attracted people from nearby villages. This trading heart of the town is shown in the painting by Patty Townsend (Figure 7).

---

17   Veasey, p. 42.

However, as the population of the town expanded in the eighteenth and nineteenth centuries, living conditions in the cramped courts that were built along Abbey Street became increasingly squalid, with appalling standards of hygiene and public health leading to high rates of infectious disease (including cholera), ill-health and death. It was in this location and in this environment that Polly Button was born, lived, worked and died.

Silk Ribbon Weaving – The Essential Backdrop

INTRODUCTION – THE HISTORICAL
DEVELOPMENT OF SILK RIBBON WEAVING

From an economy based on farming at the Norman Conquest, the town's slow, sometimes uncertain, growth was accompanied by the local development of extractive industries, specifically coal mining, brick making and quarrying. However, it was the rise of the silk ribbon trade in the area that triggered the rapid growth of the town and which provides a very dark but critical backdrop to the story of Polly Button.

Silk weaving in England developed in the late Middle Ages and had its origins in London, with records existing from the reign of Henry VI, including legislation (1455, 1463 and 1482) giving statutory protection through a ban on the importation of foreign silk – suggesting that even in its earliest days, silk weaving required state protection. Religious persecution played a large part in the early development of the industry, with Protestants being driven from the Netherlands and France in the late sixteenth century and bringing much-needed expertise with them. The silk ribbon industry in England received a further boost as a consequence of the revocation of the Edict of Nantes in France in 1685 and the destruction of Huguenot churches, as well as the closing of Protestant schools. Subsequently, many Protestants – estimates range from 210,000 to 900,000 – left France over the next two decades, with an estimated 50,000 deciding to seek refuge in England. They left without money but took with them many skills and new ideas that they used to establish small, dynamic businesses and revitalise a range of indigenous industries, including silk weaving. Initially settling in Spitalfields and Bethnal Green in London, the Huguenots played a major part in improving and extending silk manufacturing in the capital and then proceeded to expand their trade into various provincial towns, of which Coventry was one.

Coventry, like other cities that adopted the silk trade, had an earlier manufacturing base for woven goods which provided the basis for the progression to general silk weaving and, ultimately, ribbon weaving. The woollen cloth trade in Coventry had been in general decline since the sixteenth century, so the expansion into silk and ribbon weaving provided much needed employment. A silk weaving company was established in Coventry by 1627 and the trade appears to have then spread more widely to Bedworth, Nuneaton and the surrounding villages. The earliest recorded silk weaver in Nuneaton is William Oswin, who died in 1659 and whose probate inventory listed: *'all the implements in the Shop belonging to his trade and worke made and silke Redy to worke up in the house: £37.'* The first probate inventory of a Nuneaton inhabitant to specifically mention silk ribbon weaving was that of Andrew Randall who died on Christmas Day, 1662.[18]

A major silk ribbon weaving establishment in Coventry was set up by a Mr Thomas Bird in around 1703, probably assisted by other French Huguenot refugees. Other silk merchants began to set up firms in Coventry. They became wealthy in the process and were known by the locals as 'the Great Masters'. This phase marked the start of a rapid growth in ribbon weaving in the area, with Coventry at its centre and expanding silk ribbon weaving communities in its outer parishes and districts to the north, including Nuneaton.

Ribbon weaving as an industry generally prospered throughout the eighteenth century and early nineteenth century as the use of ribbons grew enormously, becoming an essential element of fashionable female dress and domestic decoration. The increasing use of ribbons by women throughout society followed fashion trends set by the upper-classes. This popularisation of upper-class tastes, a function of growing consumer demand,

---

18   Veasey, p. 71.

was a familiar occurrence in eighteenth century England. Consequently, Coventry and the ribbon weaving districts to the north of the city became the most important centre of silk ribbon manufacture in Britain.

Silk ribbons were used to adorn not only gowns (as waistbands, sashes, frills, and rosettes) but also blankets and gloves, to tie hair up for a ball, to lace dainty shoes, and to ornament baskets, cushions and curtains in the home. Ornately patterned household fabrics could also be decorated with ruchings (gathered ribbons), frills and rosettes. The huge increase in demand for more elaborate ribbons was to result in a manufacturing revolution in which Coventry and the surrounding area became the main hub for ribbon design and production in England. This was commented on by a visitor to Coventry, Thomas Pennant (a Welsh naturalist, traveller, writer and antiquarian) who wrote in 1782:

> *About eighty years ago, the silk manufacture of ribands was introduced here, and, for the first thirty years or so, remained in the hands of a few people, who acquired vast fortunes; since which it has extended to a great degree and is supposed to employ at least 10,000 people and has likewise spread into the neighbouring towns such as Nuneaton, and other places. Such real good results from our little vanities!* [19]

THE PROCESS AND TECHNOLOGY OF SILK RIBBON WEAVING

Ribbon could be woven on a variety of looms. The oldest and simplest ribbon weaving loom was the treadle-operated **single hand-loom** – so called because it was limited to producing one width or ribbon at a time (see Figures 8 and 9). Such looms were small and light enough to operate easily, thereby allowing an operation that was clean, fairly quiet, relatively undemanding and, if work was interrupted – as it may often have been in a family home – it did not damage the material being woven.

The small shuttle movement needed for ribbon weaving lent itself to a degree of automation using cogwheels and led to the

---

19   Pennant, p. 142.

development of **engine-looms** (first recorded use in Gdansk in the late sixteenth century, followed by Leiden in the 1620s) which, despite their name, were still hand- and foot-operated. The significance of the development of engine-looms is that such looms could weave more than one ribbon at once. The **Dutch engine-loom** was a development of the engine-loom. It was brought to London in about 1676, introduced to Coventry in about 1770[20] and, by the 1830s, was capable of weaving more than twenty-eight 'plain' ribbons at a time, though weavers rarely exceeded that number. Its use had generally spread rapidly in the early part of the nineteenth century.

The next technological development was the **Jacquard loom** (see Figure 10), a prototype of which was first demonstrated by its inventor, Joseph Marie Jacquard of Lyons, in Paris in 1801 and then developed to a finished device in 1804–5. Using replaceable punched cards to control a sequence of operations that controlled

Left: **Fig. 8**. A single hand-loom weaver at work.

Right: **Fig. 9**. An original, nineteenth century single hand-loom.

20 Fletcher, p. 5.

Fig. 10. Jacquard
loom, Herbert Art
Gallery and Museum,
Coventry.

the weaving of the fabric, it was an advance on the Dutch engine-loom in that it allowed much more elaborate 'fancy' ribbons to be woven at the same time. Jacquard looms began to be used in England from about 1820 and were introduced to Coventry in 1823, starting with five looms and rising to 209 in 1826[21] and to 600 or so by 1832.[22] The Jacquard loom has been described by one commentator as 'the loom for the capitalist' as it was more expensive to construct, was taller (needing a clearance of at least 11–12 feet) and required ancillary workers: the draughtsman who translated the design onto squared paper, and the card-stamper who punched holes in the cards as the squares dictated. The immediate effect was to create a greater variety of patterns. Manufacturers moving towards more factory-based operations were able to make efficiency gains by increasing productivity using engine-looms and, particularly, Jacquard looms.

THE EARLY ORGANISATION OF THE RIBBON WEAVING INDUSTRY

The ribbon trade had a three-tier structure, at the top of which was a small group of **master merchants** (the ribbon masters) who imported the raw silk from Mediterranean countries and, making use of warehouses both in London and the Midlands, transferred the silk by packhorse and then later by canal. By the beginning of the nineteenth century there were probably twelve or so master merchants in Coventry, four in Nuneaton

---

21   Select Committee on the Silk Trade, p. 70.
22   Bush, p. 112.

and one in Bedworth. The merchants had the silk thrown (spun) and dyed and then passed to the middle-men, known as **undertakers or master weavers**, who distributed it to groups of **journeyman weavers** who wove the ribbon and were paid two thirds of the finished price. Undertakers may have employed several weaving families to weave the silk ribbons required, with estimates suggesting an average of seven to eight families per undertaker.[23] Weaving was a cottage/domestic industry in which the whole family worked, with adults as weavers, and children and the elderly performing such tasks as silk winding, preparing the warp, shuttle-filling and picking-up. Weavers' cottages had characteristically large windows to enable as much of the fine work as possible to be done by daylight. Entry to the trade was by serving a seven-year apprenticeship, followed by a period as a journeyman weaver, after which the journeyman weaver may have aspired to buy a loom and set himself up as an undertaker/ master weaver.

Nuneaton's Expansion in the Early Decades of the Nineteenth Century

Throughout the eighteenth century, Nuneaton generally experienced slow but steady growth based on its silk ribbon weaving industry, although even this industrial base could be affected by seasonal fluctuations in demand and periodic depressions. This growth continued in the early nineteenth century, indeed with the first 30 years of the nineteenth century seeing a significant rise of more than 60% in Nuneaton's population – from 4,769 in 1801 to 7,799 in 1831.[24]

To service the needs of the growing population there was a surge in traders and commercial enterprises within the town. In what may have been the most dynamic phase of Nuneaton's commercial growth, the number of people who ran some sort of trade or business in the town almost doubled from just 98 in 1791 to 192 by 1828, with the number of different trades being

23   Searby, p. 195.
24   GB Historical GIS/University of Portsmouth; Rickman.

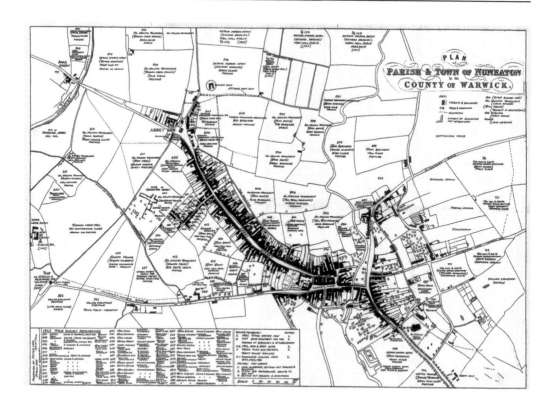

Fig. 11. Overview map of the parish and town of Nuneaton in the early 1840s, with Astley's hovel circled.

represented increasing by 27%, from 37 to 47 in little more than a generation. The principal focus of the expansion and development of the town was along Abbey Street, such that by 1828 there were almost 90 trade and commercial premises located along the street, by far the largest proportion in the town, with the next highest being in Market Place (40).[25] Polly Button's house was in a courtyard in Upper Abbey Street (Court No. 8, or Twitchell's Yard), and she and her family would have used busy and bustling Abbey Street as their main thoroughfare to and from the town centre. *Pigot & Co.'s 1828 Commercial Directory* made the following observations about Nuneaton at that time: '*The manufacture of ribbons gives employment to many hands, and is the staple trade of the place. Considerable improvements have been made within a few years in the town, the appearance of which, at a period not very distant, was by no means prepossessing.*'[26]

---

25   Barfoot & Wilkes; Pigot (1828); West; Pigot (1835).
26   Pigot, 1828, p. 828.

No maps exist from this period that show the detailed layout of the town of Nuneaton as it was. However, Figure 11 shows a detailed overview map of early 1840s Nuneaton created by Peter Lee, a local historian. The map was based on extensive research and made use of estate maps, railway plans, map fragments, the 1842 Tithe survey, and the 1888 Ordnance Survey (OS) map. The location of the barn, Astley's hovel, where Polly Button was attacked, is shown circled both in Figure 11 and in the detailed section given in Figure 12.

Readers' understanding of Nuneaton's history, its industrial and commercial growth, the town's development along Abbey Street and the surge in its population in the early nineteenth century, will be invaluable now as we begin the journey into the heart of darkness that is the true and awful story of the life and death of Polly Button.

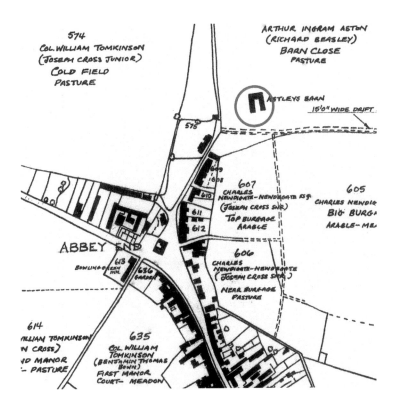

Fig. 12. Detailed section of 1840s Nuneaton map, showing Abbey End (Abbey Green) and the location of Astley's hovel (circled).

HUNGRY HEART

Polly Button and John Danks

Introduction

Fate seems to have played a hand in the relationship that brought
Polly Button and John Danks together and which ultimately
engulfed them. Polly had lived in Nuneaton all her life, while
Danks had moved into the town sometime between 1808 and
1821 after spending his early years in Astley, a few miles distant.
Both had experienced emotionally traumatic events before they
began their fateful association. Both would appear to have been
in, or have experienced, unhappy or dysfunctional relationships,
and perhaps found solace in each other. As near neighbours in
Upper Abbey Street, Nuneaton, it is likely that they would have
come into contact at one of the many local public houses, with
perhaps The Wheatsheaf on the corner of Friary Street and Upper
Abbey Street being the nearest and most likely location. We can
never know for sure what circumstances or attractions may have
drawn them together, but the evidence confirms that by 1828 the
intimate relationship that was to lead to a murderous conclusion
just four years later had begun.

Polly Button's Early Years

The mapping and confirmation of Polly Button's parents, siblings and other familial connections is made difficult by the fact that the surname of Green was one of the most common in Nuneaton in the early nineteenth century. Indeed, between 1813 and 1861 the number of baptisms of children bearing the Green family name (159) ranked second only to Smith (201) and was well ahead of the next most common, Buckler (127). This was also a time in which people were increasingly moving into urban areas in search of better pay in the new factories, so communities were in a state of considerable flux. Establishing Polly Button's genealogy therefore involved a careful analysis of entries in local parish registers for baptisms, banns, marriages and burials. To aid the research into the Green's family tree in Nuneaton, a database was created of records in the St Nicolas (Nuneaton) parish registers for baptisms (1701–1845), marriages (1701–1879) and burials (1724–1845). The database comprised a total of 920 records and proved invaluable, not only in establishing the most likely parents for Polly Button, but also confirming the difficulty of establishing her sibling relationships.

For someone tracing Polly Button's family tree the initial starting point would typically be to consider the family details presented by Cyril Marden in his book *The Murder of Polly Button*. According to Marden, Polly Button's parents were a William and Sarah Green who had raised a family of six children: Rebecca, Abraham, Hannah, Mary [Polly Button], Sarah and Thomas. However, it remains the case that only one piece of evidence exists that provides confirmation of any sibling relationship to Polly Button. This was evidence given at the trial of John Danks by the witness James Green, who gave his age as 'about twenty' and was recorded as being Polly Button's nephew. It follows therefore that James was the son of either Polly Button's brother or sister. The Greens' family tree database was used to confirm that the James Green with the closest match to this information was one baptised in the parish church of St Nicolas on 28 May 1809, the illegitimate son of a Hannah Green. Mary Green was described as being 'about forty years of age' in newspaper reports following her murder. The next step was therefore to identify any couples who may have had children named Hannah and Mary Green, with the latter being born in the few years around 1792. The records show that only two couples fall into this category: a James and Elizabeth Green and a William and Sarah Green. The pertinent details are as follows, with the most likely options highlighted.

Parents	Date of baptism of **Hannah Green**	Approx. age of **Hannah** at time of birth of James Green, c. May 1809
James/Elizabeth	16 May 1790	19y 0m
William/Sarah	9 March 1794	15y 2m

Parents	Date of baptism of **Mary Green**	Approx. age of **Mary** at time of her murder in February 1832
James/Elizabeth	25 Dec 1792	39y 2m
William/Sarah	4 Oct 1795	36y 5m

From this information it would seem that the most likely parents for Polly Button are James and Elizabeth Green. An additional piece of evidence is that Polly Button's first child was born in the house of James Green and it seems unlikely that this would have been the house of anyone other than her father. As a final consideration, the fact that this child was baptised Elizabeth might support Polly's mother being an Elizabeth rather that a Sarah.

An examination of Nuneaton's parish registers covering this period has shown that there had been two James and Elizabeth Green partnerships that could have been Polly Button's parents. The two relevant marriages had been between James Green and Elizabeth Watkins (31 January 1780) and James Green and Elizabeth Bacon (25 December 1788). Tracing back the two women involved revealed that Elizabeth Watkins had most likely been baptised on 9 January 1758 in Holy Trinity Church, Coventry, and that Elizabeth Bacon had been baptised in Nuneaton's St Nicolas Church on 11 January 1764. However, given the number and sequence of children born between 1780 and 1806 to couples comprising a James and Elizabeth Green and living in Nuneaton, it has not been possible to identify with absolute certainty which couple were Polly Button's parents, although I am inclined to the view that Polly's parents are most likely to have been James Green and Elizabeth Bacon. The uncertainty of Polly's parentage means that it has not been possible to confirm siblings for Polly Button other than Hannah.

Little is known for sure about exactly where the family lived in Nuneaton, although this is likely to have been in Abbey Street where at that time a significant proportion (almost 40%) of the town's inhabitants were concentrated and where, in due course, a number of ribbon weaving factories were to be sited. The population of Nuneaton had been rising rapidly in the early years of the nineteenth century as workers sought employment in the burgeoning ribbon weaving industry in the town. They all too often lived in squalid and fetid housing conditions in the ribbon development that took place along the length of Abbey Street.

Polly Button's Partners and Children

Between 1814 and 1829 Polly Button gave birth to five children, all of whom had different fathers. Although the initial press coverage of the murder made disparaging remarks about Polly Button's background ('...*the victim of her own gross immorality...*' and her children '*the fruit of an almost indiscriminate intercourse*')[27] only one newspaper explicitly referred to her as a prostitute.[28]

We can never know if her relationships in these instances were initially either amorous or financial in nature, as she may have turned to prostitution to provide for her young family due to poverty and severe depressions in the silk weaving trade. This issue is covered in more detail in Annexe 1 – Polly Button, Prostitute?

It seems that Polly suffered an unusually tragic sequence of events in her relationships with men. With the exception of John Danks, all but one of those that were identified as fathers in

---

27   *Leamington Spa Courier*, 25 March 1832.
28   *Leicester Chronicle*, 7 April 1832.

filiation (bastardy) orders died young. The maintenance payments that had been ordered under the Poor Law would have stopped, severely damaging Polly Button's ability to provide for her young family.

PARTNER NO. 1 – DANIEL WAGSTAFF

In the autumn of 1813, when Polly Button was twenty years old, she became pregnant for the first time as a result of a relationship with Daniel Wagstaff, the youngest son of a local well-to-do gentleman in Nuneaton, also called Daniel Wagstaff. Daniel Wagstaff Snr was an upstanding and respectable citizen, having been included in Jurors' Lists[29] for the town between 1775 and 1818 listed variably as a constable, victualler, yeoman, inn keeper (listed elsewhere as the licensee of The Bell and Fleur de Lys, Bond Street, Nuneaton, in 1806), butcher and farmer. Land tax records for 1780–89[30] also confirm that he was a man of means, owning or occupying land in Nuneaton (Market Street and Abbey End) and Attleborough. In March 1790, he paid £7 for pew seat number 19 in the south gallery of Nuneaton church, a considerable sum for the time and indicative of his comparative wealth and status in the community.[31] As a widower, he had married Elizabeth King in St Nicolas Church, Nuneaton, in July 1771, and she had born him ten children between 1772 and 1800. Daniel Wagstaff Jnr was the youngest son, born in early 1793 and baptised at St Nicolas Church, Nuneaton, on 19 February that year.

The background to how the relationship between Polly Button and Wagstaff began is unknown. Wagstaff would have been only slightly older than Polly at the time and would have been quite a catch for her, given the standing of the Wagstaff family in the locality. Polly Button's pregnancy arose during the 'big purl time' (1813–15), where demand for a particular type of fashionable

---

29 Warwickshire County Record Office, Warwickshire Jurors' Lists (Jury Books 1772-1824), QS76/3.
30 Warwickshire County Record Office. Warwickshire Land Tax Assessments (1773-1832), QS77/172/1-54.
31 Warwickshire County Record Office, Agreement to Rent Pew No. 19 in St Nicolas Parish Church, DR925/78.

ribbon led to wages rising rapidly to very high levels. Polly Button no doubt would have shared the optimism prevalent in the town, with hopes or expectations that marriage might ultimately be an outcome of their relationship. We will never know for sure what the nature or extent of that relationship may have been. Wagstaff was a young man from a well-respected and wealthy family who may have had a casual approach in his relationships with women. Equally, he may have had genuine feelings for Polly Button but may have had pressure exerted on him by his family not to marry beneath his station, which she most certainly would have been. However, for whatever reason, a proposal of marriage was not forthcoming.

Although it was not uncommon at this time for couples to wed when the woman was pregnant, unfortunately for Polly Button, as her pregnancy advanced in 1814, young Daniel still refused to marry her. On 15 June 1814, Polly gave birth to her first child, a daughter, at the house of James Green in Nuneaton. The child was baptised Elizabeth the following day at St Nicolas Church, with the entry in the parish register clearly marked '*Illegitimate*'. Given her understandable desire to have stability and security for herself and her new daughter, we can only surmise what arguments and pleas took place between Polly Button and Daniel. Unfortunately, it would all be to no avail – he would not marry her. This fateful outcome marked the beginning of Polly Button's 'undoing', her life prospects being shown to unravel from this point onwards. So, what would have happened to Polly in such circumstances? In addition to the potential social stigma of being an unmarried mother, there would be the anguish and uncertainty of how she would manage to care for the child after it had been born. Overseers of the Poor Law would also be concerned about the financial burden of the child becoming chargeable to Nuneaton parish. Under the Bastardy Act of 1576, Justices of the Peace, on the application of either the mother or parish officers, were empowered to examine the circumstances of the birth of an illegitimate child who was, or was likely to become, chargeable to the parish. Following the examination, heavy pressure would be exerted on the father to financially maintain the child and enter into a bastardy bond agreeing to pay the churchwarden and the overseers for the child's maintenance. The terms of maintenance lasted until the child was old enough to be apprenticed out. If the father resisted signing the bastardy bond, the parish officials could apply to the Justices of the Peace for a filiation order which forced him to pay for the upkeep of the child.

It appears to have been the case that Wagstaff was not willing to take any responsibility at all for Elizabeth, as just three months after her birth the Justices of the Peace made a filiation order on 13 September 1814. It adjudged Daniel Wagstaff Jnr to be the reputed father of Elizabeth (*'he did beget the said bastard child on the body of the said Mary Green'*). He was ordered to pay £2 8s for the lying in of Mary Green, i.e. when she had the baby, for the care and maintenance of Elizabeth to the time of making the filiation order, and for the expense of summoning him to the court. He was also ordered to pay 3s weekly thereafter.[32] We can only assume that Wagstaff went on to pay the money due under the filiation order, as there are no further Poor Law records that pertain to him. He certainly continued to be a man of means as the decade progressed, as in Daniel Wagstaff Snr's will, dated 8 January 1818 (less than a month before he died), some £200 in cash had been left to his namesake son. Along with his siblings, Daniel Jnr also benefited from the sale of properties and land as detailed in his father's will.[33]

However, and unfortunately for Polly Button, Daniel Wagstaff Jnr himself died only six years after his father, on 11 May 1824[34], just a few months after his 31st birthday. Wagstaff's maintenance payments would therefore have ceased, potentially throwing Polly Button and her young family into considerable distress.

PARTNER NO. **2** – JOSEPH STANTON

After her failed relationship with Daniel Wagstaff, and when her daughter Elizabeth was about 3½ years old, Polly gave birth in Nuneaton to her only son, William Green, on 25 January 1818. William's father was Joseph Stanton, who had been born in Austrey,

---

32 Warwickshire County Record Office, Filiation Order (Daniel Wagstaff) DR 280/50/60.

33 Diocese of Lichfield Wills and Probate (1776–1820), p. 499.

34 *Leicester Chronicle*, 22 May 1824, p. 3.

Warwickshire, close to the border with Derbyshire, Staffordshire and Leicestershire and some 13 miles distant from Nuneaton, in the early summer of 1783. He was therefore almost ten years older than Polly Button and, once again, we cannot be certain of the nature of the liaison between them. For reasons unknown, it was to be four years after William's birth that a filiation order was sought by the Overseers of the Poor Law. Perhaps it had been the case that Stanton had stopped regular payments agreed between the pair for the maintenance of his child. The order was made on 22 January 1822 and adjudged Joseph Stanton, whose occupation was given as a wheelwright, to be the reputed father of the bastard child William ('*now chargeable on the parish*'). Stanton was ordered to pay £2 18s 6d for the 'lying in' of Mary Green and for the care of her son, William, to the time of making the order and 2s weekly thereafter. The order made, and with two young children to support, Polly Button must have thought that her situation was set to improve. Fate, however, dealt her the first of a series of cruel blows. Two devastating words can be seen written on the reverse of the filiation order: '*Man Dead*'.[35] Research shows that Joseph Stanton had died a few months after the order had been made and had been buried on 23 June 1822 at Holy Trinity Church, Coventry. Polly Button and her children therefore continued to be in dire straits.

PARTNER NO. 3 – THOMAS BELL

Some 18 months after giving birth to William, Polly Button became pregnant again in the summer of 1819. Her third child, Hannah, was born in Polly's own house on 5 March 1820 and was baptised two days later in Nuneaton's St Nicolas Parish Church, the register again confirming the child as illegitimate. It was to be a filiation order obtained some four years later, on 11 October 1824, that reveals to us the name of the father, Thomas Bell.

The son of John and Ann Bell of Nuneaton, Thomas Bell was baptised on 23 February 1795 at St Nicolas Church. On 1

---

35 Warwickshire County Record Office, Filiation Order (Joseph Stanton) DR 280/59/4B.

July 1809, aged 14, he was apprenticed to Mary Benton, who ran a tannery business in Nuneaton. Children were likely to be apprenticed for two main reasons: either one or both parents had died, and/or the family had become impoverished. Apprenticeships relieved the Poor Law guardians of bearing the cost of supporting children in such unfortunate circumstances. Whatever his subsequent circumstances and means as an adult, Thomas formed a relationship with Polly in his mid-twenties and the birth of Hannah resulted. There does not appear to be a reason recorded as to why the filiation order was granted some four years after the birth. One can surmise that Thomas may have agreed to informal maintenance payments following the birth but circumstances, perhaps one of the periodic depressions that hit Nuneaton's weaving trade, restricted his ability to continue doing so. Given the relatively small lump sum ordered to be paid (6d), it may be that maintenance payments had continued until the summer of 1824 and that Polly's desperation – now having three children to provide for – triggered the application for a filiation order. In addition to the lump sum *'for and towards the lying in of the said Mary Green and the maintenance of the said bastard child to the time of the making of this Order'*, Bell was also ordered to pay 1s 6d weekly thereafter in maintenance payments for Hannah.[36]

Unfortunately for Polly Button, Bell was to die just four years after the order was made and was buried at St Nicolas Parish Church on 29 December 1828. Yet another important means of support for Polly's growing family had been removed.

PARTNER NO. 4 – BENJAMIN MALLABONE

The mid-1820s saw Polly strike up a relationship with Benjamin Mallabone, who was to be the father of Polly's fourth child, Ann. Benjamin had been born in 1802, the fifth child of John and Mary Mallabone, and had been baptised in St Nicolas Parish Church on 5 November of that year. The times must have been difficult for the Mallabone family, as when Benjamin was only 11 years old he

36 Warwickshire County Record Office, Filiation Order (Thomas Bell) DR280/59/43.

was apprenticed to James Mallabone, a cordwainer (shoemaker) in Birmingham, the apprenticeship indenture being dated 26 October 1812.[37]

It would seem likely that Benjamin lived at James Mallabone's shoe-making premises in Wharf Street, Birmingham, and no doubt returned home from time-to-time to visit his family in Nuneaton. It may have been as a result of one of these visits that Polly became pregnant in the spring of 1825. Mallabone would have been in his early 20's and appears to have had no intention of marrying Polly. Ann Green, Polly's third daughter, was born on 30 January 1826 at Polly Button's own house, and baptised, somewhat later than usual, on 6 August 1826 at St Nicolas Parish Church. Whatever discussions and arguments took place between Polly and Mallabone, there was no proposal of marriage and no informal arrangement to support the child. Just over a week after the baptism, on 15 August 1826, a filiation order was sought and obtained. The order adjudged Benjamin Mallabone, '*late of the parish of Nuneaton, cordwainer*', to be the reputed father of the bastard child. The insertion of the word 'late' confirms that he was no longer living in Nuneaton at this time. The order required Mallabone to pay £2 3s 6d for the lying in of Polly and for the maintenance of the child to that date, and thereafter to pay 2s 8d weekly.[38] There are no further Poor Law records pertaining to Benjamin Mallabone, so it may have been the case that he continued to make the maintenance payments. However, his continued residence in Birmingham, more than 20 miles away, might have presented some difficulties in continuity and enforcement of payments.

Somewhat tragically for Polly Button, it can now be seen that between 1822 and 1828, the fathers of three of her children had unfortunately all died at a relatively young age, when compared to the average male life expectancy of the time which has been estimated to have been about 40 years.[39] The sequence of early deaths had been as follows: Joseph Stanton, aged 38, in 1822;

---

37 Warwickshire County Record Office, Apprenticeship Indenture for Benjamin Mallabone DR280/83/33.

38 Warwickshire County Record Office, Filiation Order (Benjamin Mallabone) DR280/50/60.

39 Davenport, p. 28.

Daniel Wagstaff, aged 30, in 1824, and then Thomas Bell, aged 34, in 1828. All had been required to make maintenance payments under filiation orders and all such payments would have stopped upon their death. Benjamin Mallabone continued to live in Birmingham.

Enter John Danks: Partner No. 5

It is at this point in Polly's unfortunate series of relationships with men that John Danks first appears on the scene, becoming the fifth person to father a child with her. We can trace Danks's own story through relevant parish records and from an examination of Danks by two Justices of the Peace in Warwick on Saturday 25 February 1832, one week after he had murdered Polly Button. The examination interview was undertaken at Petty Sessions held at the Judges' House, Warwick, near to the gaol where he was held after his arrest for the murder.[40]

DANKS'S EARLY YEARS AND EMPLOYMENT HISTORY

Danks was the second of four sons born to Thomas and Elizabeth Danks in Astley, a small village located five miles southwest of Nuneaton. Born in 1787, he was baptised on 14 October of that year in the parish church of St Mary the Virgin, by the Rev B. G. Ebdell, who had been presented by the Crown as vicar the previous year. Of passing interest is the fact that Ebdell would later baptise Mary Ann Evans (George Eliot) at Chilvers Coton Church in November 1819. Danks lived with his family in Astley and worked for his father until he was sixteen years of age. His first recorded employment was in 1803, when he worked for Isaac Pearson of Astley for one year under a weekly hiring. Danks then spent a couple of years working for John Clarke, a farmer in Chilvers Coton near Nuneaton. This was followed by a year working for James Morris of Griff, Chilvers Coton, before returning to the employment of the Pearson family, being hired

---

40   Warwickshire County Record Office, The Examination of John Danks DR280/56/98A.

by Isaac Pearson the Elder in September 1807 to serve his son Isaac Pearson the Younger at his farm in Fillongley. The following year, Danks returned to working for Isaac Pearson the Elder on his farm at Astley Hall. In the early years of his working life Danks had therefore had at least three spells of employment with the Pearson family. The Pearsons were a relatively prosperous family of farmers who had worked the land for generations in and around Fillongley, five miles from Nuneaton and had risen to become yeomen, owning their land rather than renting it from a local landholder. Interestingly, his employment with the Pearson family provides a connection to Nuneaton's famous novelist George Eliot through her mother, Christiana, who was the daughter of Isaac Pearson the Elder.

Danks's employment record as detailed in his examination contains no further details of specific hirings. From the examination document itself, which refers to Danks as a labourer, and from evidence presented at the trial and covered by the press, it would appear that Danks had continued to work as an agricultural labourer until the time of the murder. One local newspaper was later to report that Danks had been a '*hedge carpenter and rather an ingenious man at his business*'.[41] A 'hedge carpenter' was a recognised craftsman, able to create a variety of useful wooden items, for example tools, farm implements and furniture, more often than not finding many of the shapes he needed for his products growing naturally.

DANKS'S MARITAL HISTORY AND CHILDREN

In early 1803, banns had been read out for Danks's intended marriage to Sarah Ward at St Mary the Virgin Parish Church, Astley, but the marriage was delayed for some reason and did not take place until 11 March 1805, with Rev Ebdell again officiating. Their first child, Ann, was born a few months later and was baptised on 25 August 1805 at St Mary's, Astley. Their second and final child, a boy also bearing the name John Danks, followed three years later. In due course, the family settled in Abbey Street,

---

41   *Leamington Spa Courier*, 7 April 1832, p. 3.

Nuneaton, but unfortunately Sarah Danks died at the age of 48 in June 1821, leaving behind Danks and two children in their mid- to late-teens. However, it took Danks less than a year to find a partner for himself and a mother for his children, as on 12 May 1822 he married Jane Floyde, a widow of less than three years, in Nuneaton's parish church. The marriage was to be childless, as Floyde's first marriage had been.

It became evident at the trial of John Danks that he had been living near to Polly Button in Abbey Street and had begun a relationship with her. As with Polly Button's four previous partners, we have no way of knowing for sure what lay behind the relationship, but the necessity of providing for her young family of four growing children is likely to have driven impoverished Polly towards prostitution. This would appear to have been a common occurrence in this period, especially in view of the regularity of economic recessions and the transience of paid employment. Equally, it may also have been the case that Danks provided some desperately needed love and affection. Whatever the reason for the liaison, it was in late 1828 or early 1829 that Polly became pregnant again. This coincided with the death of Thomas Bell, the father of her daughter Hannah, who had been buried on 29 December 1828. No doubt this loss reinforced how isolated and exposed Polly Button had become. There were now no fathers alive or living locally obliged to pay maintenance for any of her children – she was completely at the mercy of the Poor Law guardians. On 21 September 1829, her daughter, Jane, was born, with her baptism following on 29 September at the parish church of St Nicolas. Polly must have been desperate to secure maintenance for the child, as less than a month later a filiation order against John Danks was secured. Dated 27 October 1829, the order adjudged Danks, listed as a labourer, to be the father of the child. In addition to being ordered to pay 6s for the costs of obtaining the filiation order, Danks was also ordered to pay 1s 6d weekly thereafter as maintenance as long as the child was chargeable to the parish of Nuneaton. Danks was also ordered to pay 4s for the reasonable charges and expenses related to the child's birth and a further 4s 6d for the costs of apprehending him and securing his attendance at the hearing. This latter charge means that Danks must have been reluctant to acknowledge his responsibility for the child, resulting as it did in his arrest and being brought before the Justices. In addition to the required weekly payments, the one-off costs incurred by Danks therefore amounted to 16s 6d.[42]

Evidence given at the murder trial indicated that Danks and Polly Button had continued to have an on-going relationship after Jane had been born, with witnesses confirming that they had seen the pair going for walks together over the burgage fields towards Astley's barn. Living in such close proximity resulted in evident antipathy between Polly and Danks's wife, Jane. Arguments between John Danks, his wife and Polly Button were widely known about in the neighbourhood and were commented on by witnesses at the trial. It is also possible that Jane Danks's dislike might well have been made worse when Polly Button gave the name Jane to her fifth child, perhaps rubbing salt into the wound of Polly's continuing relationship with her husband. The fateful consequence of the on-going liaison with John Danks was that Polly became pregnant again, for the sixth time, in the autumn of 1831. Fearful of her family's situation in the increasingly dire economic circumstances affecting Nuneaton at that time, Polly Button sought a filiation order against Danks in relation to the unborn child. A warrant for bastardy before birth was subsequently granted on 31 January 1832.[43] In it, the constable for Nuneaton was instructed to apprehend Danks immediately and bring him before the Justices with the intention of indemnifying the parish of Nuneaton for the costs associated with the forthcoming birth and the upbringing of the child. Less than two weeks later the Justices were in action again regarding Danks. The overseers of the poor for Nuneaton had made a complaint that Danks had not abided by the order of bastardy that had been issued in October 1829 and that he now owed £4 8s 6d that should have been paid for the support and maintenance of his daughter, Jane. Given that he had been ordered to pay 1s 6d a week, this would seem to indicate that he had stopped paying the required maintenance at least 42

---

42 Warwickshire County Record Office, Filiation Order (John Danks) DR280/59/80.

43 Warwickshire County Record Office, Warrant for Bastardy Before Birth (John Danks) DR280/89.

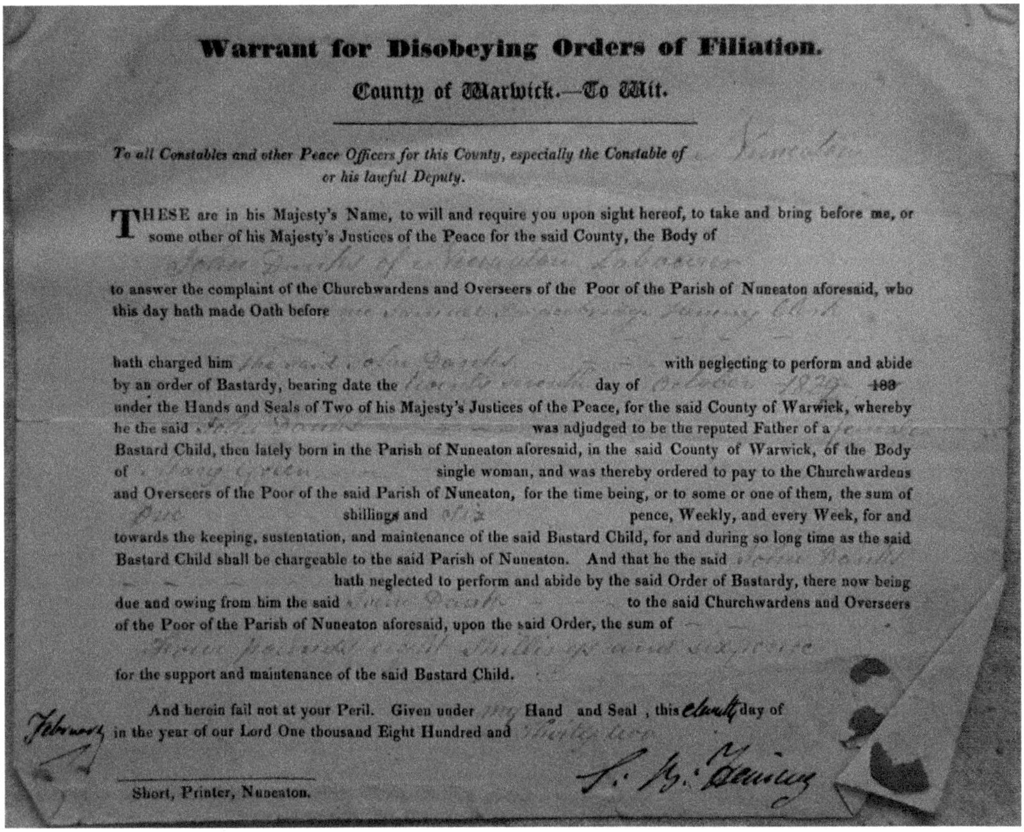

Warrant for Disobeying Orders of Filiation.

County of Warwick.—To Wit.

To all Constables and other Peace Officers for this County, especially the Constable of _____
or his lawful Deputy.

THESE are in his Majesty's Name, to will and require you upon sight hereof, to take and bring before me, or some other of his Majesty's Justices of the Peace for the said County, the Body of

to answer the complaint of the Churchwardens and Overseers of the Poor of the Parish of Nuneaton aforesaid, who this day hath made Oath before

hath charged him _____ with neglecting to perform and abide by an order of Bastardy, bearing date the _____ day of _____ 18— under the Hands and Seals of Two of his Majesty's Justices of the Peace, for the said County of Warwick, whereby he the said _____ was adjudged to be the reputed Father of a _____ Bastard Child, then lately born in the Parish of Nuneaton aforesaid, in the said County of Warwick, of the Body of _____ single woman, and was thereby ordered to pay to the Churchwardens and Overseers of the Poor of the said Parish of Nuneaton, for the time being, or to some or one of them, the sum of _____ shillings and _____ pence, Weekly, and every Week, for and towards the keeping, sustentation, and maintenance of the said Bastard Child, for and during so long time as the said Bastard Child shall be chargeable to the said Parish of Nuneaton. And that he the said _____ hath neglected to perform and abide by the said Order of Bastardy, there now being due and owing from him the said _____ to the said Churchwardens and Overseers of the Poor of the Parish of Nuneaton aforesaid, upon the said Order, the sum of _____

for the support and maintenance of the said Bastard Child.

And herein fail not at your Peril. Given under _____ Hand and Seal, this _____ day of _____ in the year of our Lord One thousand Eight Hundred and _____

Short, Printer, Nuneaton.

Fig. 13. Warrant for the apprehension of John Danks for disobeying the order of filiation relating to his daughter, Jane Green, born 1829. The warrant was issued on 11 February 1832, just one week before Danks was to murder Polly Button.

weeks previously. In the chaos that had enveloped Nuneaton's Poor Law system in the years leading up to 1831–32 (see Chapter 4, 'Badlands', and Annexe 2 – The Historical Background), it would appear that Danks's non-payment of maintenance had not been noticed by the Poor Law officers. On Saturday 11 February 1832, the Justices issued a warrant for disobeying the order of filiation.[44] Instructions were given '*to all Constables and other Peace Officers for this County, especially the Constable of Nuneaton*' for Danks to be brought before the Justices to answer the complaint of the parish officials.

This must have thrown Danks into a desperate panic. With the industrial and economic collapse in Nuneaton at that time wreaking havoc and leading to destitution throughout the town,

44   Warwickshire County Record Office, Warrant for Disobeying Orders of Filiation (John Danks) DR280/90.

Danks must have felt his situation was helpless, as he possessed little if any means to pay this significant debt. The bitterness that his wife felt towards Polly Button would be made even worse. Did Danks's wife know about the debt that had built up and was about to be revealed? Or had Danks kept that debt a secret from his wife and was it all now about to unravel for him? Danks must have felt trapped and was no doubt desperately searching for ways out of his terrible predicament. The next few days would see Danks make a fateful decision, one that would set him on the path to the gallows.

BADLANDS

Nuneaton In Early 1832:
Desperate Times, Desperate People

Introduction

As the fateful relationship between Polly Button and John Danks approached its catastrophic conclusion in the winter of 1831–32, the couple's dismal outlook was mirrored in the appalling state of affairs that now prevailed in Nuneaton. The town had prospered in the late eighteenth century and early nineteenth century on the back of its silk ribbon weaving industry. The vast majority of its population became either directly or indirectly dependent on the trade for employment. However, by the early 1830s the town found itself in a perilous position, devastated by the collapse of the silk trade and struggling to survive the severe and sustained depression that followed. But how had conditions deteriorated to such an extent over a single generation, why had they accelerated in the few years previously, and what would the conditions in the town actually have been like in those calamitous times? An understanding of the significant and rapid changes that took place within the silk ribbon weaving industry, and the severe impact of these changes on the lives of those living in ribbon weaving communities, will help answer these questions. It will also reveal the dreadful conditions that prevailed in the town at that time, conditions that would have been directly experienced by Polly

Button and John Danks and contributed in no small way to the spiral of poverty and despair that led to Polly's bloody and violent death.

Silk Ribbon Weaving in Nuneaton – Growth, Dependence and Collapse

THE RIBBON TRADE IN THE PERIOD LEADING UP TO 1826

Fluctuations in demand for silk ribbons could be both frequent and considerable, and arose primarily because of the following:

- The pace and extent of changing fashions – exerting perhaps the most persistent influence on demand, with extensive sales in one season sometimes being followed by falling consumption in the next.
- As a ribbon would never be a purchase out of necessity, when economic conditions deteriorated so did the demand for ribbons.
- The seasonality of the trade, with demand for ribbons being greatest in the summer and at its lowest in the winter.

The peak of ribbon weaving in Nuneaton occurred during the 'big purl time', which lasted from February 1813 to the close of the Napoleonic Wars in November 1815. In this period of great prosperity, there was a sudden fashion and huge demand for ribbons with wide purl edges, known as picot-edged ribbons, that had decorative scallop loops along the sides. Manufacturers had difficulty keeping up with demand and during this period could charge almost any price they chose to ask for their goods. With 20–25% of men away serving in the army fighting Napoleon's forces, manufacturers competed against each other for the available labour, and wages rose to an extraordinary level.

However, this dramatic increase in trade and prosperity was not to last. The big purl time ended abruptly with a sudden collapse in demand for purl-edged ribbons. The Napoleonic Wars ended with the Second Treaty of Paris in 1815, and soldiers returning from the battlefield re-entered the labour market. This caused a significant downward pressure on wages at the same time as food prices were increasing dramatically after a sequence of bad harvests in Europe caused by the enormous eruption of Mount Tambora in Indonesia in April 1815, one of the most powerful in recorded history. Along with other ribbon weaving communities across the country, Nuneaton's ribbon weavers found themselves in impoverished circumstances as a result.

The various parties in the ribbon weaving industry in the following twenty years or so were locked in an increasingly desperate struggle for survival. There were unsuccessful attempts to introduce and maintain uniform lists of prices for woven goods and an increase in disputes about the introduction of new technology and wages which led to social unrest and strikes. The first local strike was recorded in Coventry in 1819, followed by further strikes in 1822 and 1831. Undertakers, or master weavers, were encouraged by the ribbon wholesalers of London and Manchester, anxious to defend their profits by cutting out the middlemen ribbon masters, to set up as manufacturers ('little masters') on their own. In response, the ribbon masters sought their security in cutting out the undertakers and giving work directly to journeymen. In this way, in just a few years, three quarters of the engine-loom trade was removed from the undertaking system, which survived only in the rural parishes to the north of Coventry, including Nuneaton. There was a general abandonment of the list of prices for woven ribbons, while 'honourable' masters who wished to continue to pay by it found themselves defeated by the cut-throat actions of their competitors. The lower the weaver's position in this functional hierarchy, the worse was his fate during the decline. Journeyman weavers working single hand-looms in domestic settings were worst affected of all. Unfortunately for Nuneaton, most of its weavers fell into this category.

THE REMOVAL OF PROHIBITION AND THE CATASTROPHIC EFFECT
ON THE RIBBON TRADE IN NUNEATON (1826–1832)

A prohibition on the importation of foreign woven silk goods had been in place since 1766. In addition, the Spitalfields Acts of 1773, 1792 and 1811 had established price and wage controls that sought to protect the weavers and manufacturers of Spitalfields in a home-based monopoly. Cocooned in such a protected market there was little incentive for, or action taken by, ribbon manufacturers to improve their machinery. The same old-fashioned looms continued to be used and there was only a slow uptake of the more advanced and more efficient Jacquard looms. Little or no action was taken to improve the quality, appeal or design of ribbons, to review production methods and efficiencies, to respond more quickly to the demands of rapidly-changing fashions, or to train and develop designers as they had in France. However, in the post-Napoleonic War period there was a significant movement in support of free trade in Europe. Consequently, free trade legislation was passed in 1824, with a two-year lead-in period, that repealed the prohibition on foreign silks and swept away price and wage controls in the industry. This change was to be the cause of a further and irrevocable collapse in ribbon weaving in Nuneaton.

It became apparent that manufacturers did not take advantage of the opportunity presented by the two-year lead-in period. As Benjamin Poole, a witness from Coventry, stated when asked by the Select Committee on the Silk Trade in 1832 if any improvements had taken place in the manufacture of ribbons in Coventry: '*Not in the last three, four or five years, or beyond that time, I do not remember any that have taken place within seven years. The machinery we have now in use, was in use prior to that time, for a considerable length of time.*'[45]

French ribbons remained the most sought after because of their superior quality and design. As a consequence, they had continued to be smuggled in during the period of prohibition to meet the established preference and demand of higher-class consumers.[46] Local manufacturers could not match the quality and designs of the ribbons produced in France. The deficiency in local machines was notable: the highest Jacquard machine 'numbers' (of needles which guide the warp threads) in St Etienne were about 1,050 (although 900 was common, as also were 600 and 400) while in Coventry the highest was 600, and the greater number 400, with some 250.[47] This continental productive

---

45   Select Committee on the Silk Trade, p. 52.
46   Fletcher, p. 12.
47   Searby, p. 98.

advantage was also supplemented by a strong focus on, and investment in, art and design skills within the industry. For example, by 1840 there were 58 artists at St. Etienne ('the Coventry of France') employed in the production of ribbon patterns.[48] Unfortunately, there was no Coventry or Warwickshire equivalent of the school of design in Lyon with its 180 students taking a five-year course, with the consequence that local designs were often made by imitating French patterns in an attempt to catch the market.

Foreign competition following the end of prohibition merely worsened the underlying problem in the ribbon trade, one of excess of both looms and labour. When French ribbon manufacturers began to compete seriously in the British market, the prosperity of the ribbon masters ceased, and weavers, already poor, became poorer still, to the point of destitution. By 1828, French manufacturers had established successful distribution networks for their ribbons and sent enormous quantities of both plain and fancy ribbons to England. As regards the former, such ribbons were the mainstay of Nuneaton's production, given the limitations of the type of loom predominant in the town, so the consequences were particularly acute. One Nuneaton manufacturer, William Jacombs, complained in 1829 that he and his partner had found that French ribbons were so rapidly circulating through the country that this had caused them to lose the customer base they had built up through extensive travelling to most of the towns of England.[49] It would seem that their business never recovered, as in February 1833 they were both declared bankrupt.[50]

Despite the retention of import duties of 25–40% on silks, foreign-manufactured ribbons were still much cheaper than those produced in Coventry and Warwickshire. Swiss ribbons declined further still in price (10–20%) between 1827 and 1832, while in the same period French ribbon prices dropped by 25%. The Select Committee on the Silk Trade in 1832 heard evidence from a Coventry ribbon manufacturer that English articles were 78% more expensive than French ones on average, with labour

---

48 Fletcher, p. 22.
49 Select Committee on the Silk Trade, p. 84.
50 *London Gazette*, 12 February 1833.

costs being some 108% higher.[51] The pressure to compete with continental producers resulted in a disastrous decline in the rate of payments to weavers in Warwickshire from 1828 onwards. Many fancy weavers were forced to abandon their craft when this segment of the Warwickshire trade was affected and turn instead to plain weaving, which required less time and skill and therefore paid much less. The competition of weavers with each other in the plain trade, now more overcrowded than ever, enabled or forced manufacturers to cut wage rates still further.

In Nuneaton, the distress led to a massive increase in the number of claimants on the poor rate and an alarming reduction in the number of contributors to it. Distress funds and soup kitchens were established locally in response. The dire circumstances of silk weavers throughout the country in the late 1820s and the early 1830s resulted in the establishment of a Select Committee on the Silk Trade in 1832. This was followed by a Parliamentary Select Committee on petitions from the hand-loom weavers (reporting in 1834 and 1835) and a Royal Commission on Hand-loom Weavers, established in 1837 and issuing a number of reports up to 1841. Much of the detail of the widespread poverty and hardship arising from the collapse of the ribbon weaving trade in Coventry and Warwickshire comes from these reports. They all clearly illustrate the appalling social and economic consequences for the area, with Nuneaton being particularly badly affected because of specific factors relating to the structure and practice of the ribbon weaving industry in the town.

The removal of prohibition therefore had a particularly damaging impact on the ribbon weaving industry in Coventry and Warwickshire, with Nuneaton suffering more than anywhere else. It led to the development of a hierarchy in the Coventry and Warwickshire area based on both productive capacity and geographical location, with Nuneaton in the most disadvantaged position. One author has described the local structure in 1830 as, *'rather like that of a large estate with a core of constantly cultivated fertile soil and concentric circles of increasingly marginal land round it.'*[52]

---

51   Select Committee on the Silk Trade, p. 104.
52   Searby, pp. 108–9.

In the most constant employment were the more industrialised and centralised loom-shops which had arisen very largely since the mid-1820s and which were centred in Coventry. Almost all the loom-shop looms were engine-looms, most of them were Jacquards and they were owned by the manufacturers and operated by loom-shop journeymen employees. Then came the first-hand journeymen – outdoor weavers who owned their own looms and worked at home – although they increasingly found themselves dependent on unpredictable orders from the manufacturers as demand fluctuated. At the periphery of this concentric system, both logically and topographically, were the areas to the north of Coventry, particularly Nuneaton, where single hand-looms predominated. Here, alone, the old undertaking system survived, partly because the dispersed and allegedly ill-disciplined nature of the workforce made the supervision of the undertaker necessary. In this outer, more 'barren' circle, the most weakly-capitalised of undertakers provided the most ancient and inefficient single hand-looms for an increasingly destitute and desperate workforce of men, and many more women and children. These weavers would have been the first to have been laid off as demand dropped because of their peripheral location, productive inefficiency, and the technical and design limitations of their looms.

Nuneaton – 'Not Weaving But Drowning'

Having outlined how economic and technological factors had brought Nuneaton's ribbon weaving trade to its knees by 1832, it is now worth considering how this industrial decline, at times severe and rapid, impacted on the lives of Nuneaton's inhabitants, so overwhelmingly dependent as they were on this industry as their primary source of employment. The overall impact was to bring the long-term rise in the town's population to a juddering halt and, indeed, usher in a fall in the number of inhabitants. Between 1831 and 1841, the population of Nuneaton parish fell from 7,799 to 7,105 (a decline of 9%), while the population of the wider town fell from 12,870 to 12,250 (a fall of 4.8%) – see Figure 14. Other than Atherstone, which had a slight fall in population of 0.13%, no other town in Warwickshire experienced a fall in its population in this

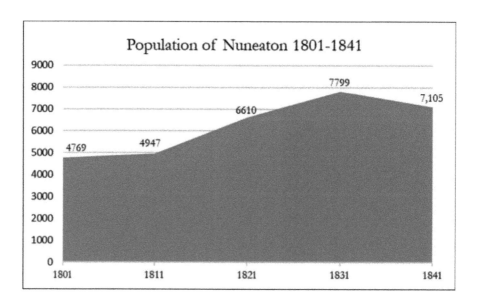

Population of Nuneaton 1801-1841

Fig. 14. Population of
Nuneaton,
1801–1841.
Source: Census
records.

decade.[53] The flight of a significant number of its inhabitants from Nuneaton provides further evidence of the uniquely severe impact the depression in the silk ribbon weaving industry had on the town.

The fall in population was mirrored by a decline in the extent of trade and commerce. Between 1828 and 1830 there was a 3.6% drop in the number of tradespeople in the town from 192 to 187. In the seven years from 1828 to 1835, various trades relying on discretionary spending were noticeably and adversely affected, for example the town's only toyshop closed down and the number of booksellers halved to leave just two. It would seem that even some of those providing staple items were not immune to the downturn, with the number of bakeries and flour dealers reducing in number from 17 to 11. Even pawnbrokers, reducing from two businesses to one, struggled to make a living. One notable exception was the number of licensed victuallers, inn keepers and retailers of beer who increased by 38% from 32 to 44. It seems that even in the depths of a depression, Nuneaton residents remained intent on drowning their sorrows.[54]

53   General Register Office.
54   Pigot (1828), West, Pigot (1835).

NUNEATON IN THE TIME OF POLLY BUTTON

A number of contemporary sources give shocking accounts of the extreme financial, social and environmental consequences for Nuneaton of the fluctuations and decline of the silk ribbon weaving industry during Polly Button's adult life. These sources can be summarised into three categories: first, details contained in a personal diary and in correspondence of the time; second, reports from government-appointed committees established to look into the severe problems that had beset the silk weaving trade in the UK; and third, a report from the General Board of Health in 1849 on the dreadful state of public health in the town.

Although some of these sources were published after Polly Button's murder, they all provide evidence of the general trend of decline, at times precipitous, in the ribbon weaving trade and the consequent destitution and poverty throughout the town. The appalling situations, experiences and conditions described within them were likely to have been at their worst perhaps in the winter of 1831–32 and would have directly impacted the daily life of Polly Button and her children. Equally, they are also likely to have been major causative factors that tipped John Danks over the edge to commit murder. These sources provide a vivid, uncompromising and desperately sad account of the state of the town in the period when Polly Button was raising her family. A summarised account of the contents of these documents as they relate to Nuneaton's predicament now follows, with a more extensive commentary provided in Annexe 2 – The Historical Background.

The most intimate portrait of the town is that contained in *The Memorandum Book of Occurrences at Nuneaton* (also known as *The Nuneaton Diary*),[55] maintained from 1810 until 1845 by John Astley, a grocer with premises in Market Place. His diary provides a unique insight into the life and times of Polly Button's Nuneaton. The diary makes frequent reference to the poor state of the ribbon weaving trade, with the years 1816–17, 1822–23 and late 1825–32 proving to be particularly difficult. The diary makes reference to bankruptcies in the town for the first time in

---

55 Astley, J.

living memory, a massive increase in poor relief, donations from a charitable society in London, and soup kitchens serving up to 1,000 gallons a week for the town's hungry and impoverished citizens. The ever-lower rates of pay for weavers led to social disturbances and, in November 1831, physical attacks on the property of local manufacturers. This escalation in the anger and desperation of local weavers triggered a rapid response from the town's Establishment, which created about 250 Special Constables and organised patrols by three nightwatchmen over the winter months. The last entry in the diary for 1831 seems to sum up the situation succinctly: '*The year 1831 was a year of great distress to the dependents on the ribbon trade. Ruin and poverty are the lot of Hundreds in this Town.*'

The damaging consequences of the depression were prolonged, being referred to in a letter written by the niece of Francis Newdigate of Arbury Hall some two years later: '*The Gwythers returned to* [Chilvers] *Coton yesterday and gave a melancholy account of the ruinous state of Nuneaton. Mr Ball who kept the draper's shop next to Mr Short, has failed, and his parents will quit Coton altogether... Mr Taylor and Mr Arnold* [perfumer, Back Street] *are expected to become Bankrupt.*'[56]

Nuneaton was not alone in suffering dreadfully from the decline in silk weaving. The widespread distress in weaving communities across the country triggered petitions to Parliament and resulted in the appointment of four committees between 1818 and 1840 to investigate the problems that had arisen. The committees conducted wide-ranging interviews with all interested parties in their attempts to understand both the causes of the industry's severe problems and the consequent desperate circumstances of the hand-loom weavers. Of the significant number of witnesses who attended the hearings to give evidence of the terrible state of affairs in silk weaving communities, there were representatives of both ribbon weavers and ribbon manufacturers in Coventry, Foleshill and Nuneaton.

---

56   Letter from Eliza Lucy Parker to Francis Newdigate (son of Francis Newdigate, of Arbury Hall), 14 December 1833 (Warwickshire County Record Office, CR0136/B4163).

The national crisis that enveloped the silk ribbon weaving industry after the end of the Napoleonic Wars led to the first government-sponsored committee report into the harsh conditions experienced by the country's ribbon weavers, published in 1818. The committee heard evidence on 24 April 1818 from William Fletcher, a weaver from Nuneaton, who had moved to the town from Coventry less than three years previously. Fletcher complained about the very low prices being paid in accordance with the 'Union List' of prices for woven goods that was used in the area. He told the committee that such low earnings were causing unprecedented levels of distress in the town and then presented figures that showed almost a doubling of the previous year's cost of poor relief payments to those in need.[57] A petition from the inhabitants of Nuneaton was also delivered that referred to the *'great distress which prevailed among the ribbon weavers in this district'*. It was also stated that almost two thirds of the town's 2,192 looms were idle in February 1817.[58]

The next government report was that of the Select Committee on the Silk Trade, which was published in August 1832, the year of Polly Button's murder. The committee had been set up to investigate concerns about the effect of the removal of the prohibition on the importation of silk goods in 1826. The main impact on the country's ribbon weaving communities had been a collapse in wages paid to weavers and the consequent widespread unemployment and destitution. Witnesses from Coventry described the significant problems affecting the city's weavers, including one who told the committee that there had been more distress in 1831 than he had ever known in Coventry before. The overwhelming majority of Coventry's weavers were using engine-looms or Jacquard looms and might earn a minimum of 7s 6d a week, about three times as much as those using single hand-looms. Such wages were for working 14–16 hours, and sometimes even up to 18 hours a day. Nuneaton's weaving community is likely to have been affected more severely than Coventry's due to the town having a much higher proportion of the less productive single hand-looms.

---

57 Committee on Ribbon Weavers (March 1818), p. 16.
58 Committee on Ribbon Weavers (April/May 1818), p 129.

'Sinking fast
in a state of
degradation'

When the post-1826 depression struck, the vast majority of looms in Nuneaton became idle due to the lack of work, with the proportion reaching more than 80% in 1831. This level of loom redundancy was the highest in the area and almost twice that of Coventry (44.8%). The committee heard harrowing tales of despair by witnesses from ribbon weaving communities. One of the weavers' representatives spoke of weavers, '*sinking fast in a state of degradation; their wants press on them in various ways, their bellies go half full, their backs half clothed, and the people feel no inclination to send their children to school; and a state of degradation and immorality is fast overtaking them.*'[59] Another witness, a ribbon manufacturer, considered the condition of the weavers to be '*wretched in the extreme*', and spoke of '*the state of degradation and the horrible misery that is inflicted on the working community*'.[60]

Evidence was given by just one witness from Nuneaton, the ribbon manufacturer William Jacombs. Jacombs gave his evidence on 28 March 1832, just over a month after Polly Button had been murdered. He informed the committee that three quarters of the town's population of 8,000 were directly involved in the ribbon trade and that there had been a great drop in wages since 1826. Soup kitchens had been set up to feed the hungry of the town and had expanded rapidly to a point where they were feeding almost 40% of the town's inhabitants. He provided figures that showed that the total expenditure on poor relief in Nuneaton parish had more than doubled from £1,999 to £4,782 between 1825 and 1832 and now stood at an unprecedented level. Equally, the number of people receiving poor relief had risen dramatically from 868 to 3,240. This 273% increase in the number of impoverished citizens was significantly higher than the increase that had occurred in 1818 and which had wreaked such havoc on that occasion. The rapid expansion of poor relief confirms the scale of the calamity that had befallen the town in the few years before Danks's murderous act.

Further insight into the continuing and terrible conditions experienced by hand-loom weavers in that period is contained in a further select committee report published in 1835. While

59   Select Committee on the Silk Trade, p. 807.
60   Ibid., p. 651.

containing general but still shocking descriptions of '*degradation, recklessness and vice*', the report also provided definitive evidence of the collapse in the wages of the weavers. This was shown dramatically in the evidence of a witness from Bolton, a town like Nuneaton in that its weaving industry was also dominated by single hand-looms. Using workhouse records from 1797–1832, the witness confirmed that there had been a fall in weavers' wages of 76% and almost the same reduction in purchasing power for essential food items. Similarly, a witness from Nuneaton suggested a decline in wages of almost the same order estimating that there had been a reduction of about two thirds. Suffice to say, the impact of such a decline in the weavers' standard of living had been severe. The report referenced a quote from the influential philosopher, William Paley: '*To an individual who has no capital except in his hands, machinery* [in the guise of the more productive engine-looms and Jacquard looms] *has, like a destroying angel, come and cut off his hands, and permitted the individual to starve by inches.*'[61] Nuneaton fared badly in comparison with other silk weaving communities, the committee recording that Nuneaton had the second lowest wage rate for weavers in England at 4s 8d per week, with Bolton's weekly rate being the only one lower at 4s 1½d. Even then, evidence elsewhere in the report suggests that weavers' wages in Nuneaton could have been nearer 2s 6d a week, with a suggestion that Bolton's weavers may have been able to earn around 6s 4d a week. Whatever the actual level of comparative average wages, it remains the case that Nuneaton's ribbon weavers were amongst the poorest paid weavers in the country.

The most comprehensive account of the deprivation amongst weavers in Coventry and Warwickshire between the years 1826 and 1840 was given in the *Assistant Hand-Loom Weavers' Commissioners' Report* of 1840 covering the Midlands, also known as the *Fletcher Report* after its author, Joseph Fletcher. The Royal Commission had been appointed in 1837 to enquire into unemployment and poverty in the textile industry. Reports were produced on a regional basis and contain a wealth of information and analysis of the silk weaving industry and the causes for its sustained and sometimes

---

61   Select Committee – Hand-Loom Weavers (August 1835), p. 19.

rapid decline over the previous thirty years or so. Fletcher's report covered the Midlands (primarily Coventry and Warwickshire) and examined the industrial, moral and physical condition of weavers in the area. In doing so, Fletcher was to identify specific reasons why Nuneaton had been so badly affected.

As regards the industrial condition, the report recorded that of the 3,200 looms in use in Nuneaton in 1838, only 200 (6.25%) had been the more efficient Jacquard looms, with the remaining 3,000 (93.75%) being the less productive single hand-looms. This put the town at a significant, if not insurmountable disadvantage, compared to Coventry where the total number of single hand-looms being used by weavers amounted to just 129, less than 3% of the total looms available there. Coventry also had a much more extensive manufacturing base that could take advantage of the greater productivity of the engine-looms and the recently introduced Jacquard looms. The comparison was stark: there were 127 silk ribbon manufacturers in Coventry compared with just four in Nuneaton. Fletcher also commented on wages received by differing classes of weavers in Coventry and Warwickshire and the devastating effect this had on living standards. He noted that, '*on entering the rural districts,* [wages] *appear to decline in proportion to the distance from the city, among each class of the operative hands respectively; and in the single-hand trade... the earnings of the journeyhands cannot be averaged at more than 5s. per week. The poverty of the remoter rural districts is painfully conspicuous in their miserable cottages, ragged children, and general squalor.*'[62] The report's section on the moral condition of the weavers provides further observations on the differences between Coventry and Nuneaton. In considering the 1830s, Fletcher contrasted the engine-weaving trade in Coventry and its suburbs – where '*superior habits and intelligence prevail*' – with '*the dispersed and ignorant inhabitants of the rural parishes* [including Nuneaton],

---

62   Fletcher, p. 327.

employed chiefly in the single hand trade and retaining most of their original barbarism with an accession of vice.'[63] Fletcher's report therefore provides further evidence for the 'decreasing concentric circles' model of ribbon weaving emanating from Coventry[64] and the consequently appalling conditions that would have been prevalent in Nuneaton in the years around Polly Button's murder.

Fletcher went on to state that he had found it hard to credit the evidence of witnesses about the '*moral debasement which prevails among the country weavers… but the overwhelming flood of evidence on every side at length compelled me to recognise a grossness and an immorality.'*[65] The lack of religious guidance and support in Nuneaton parish was noted, with the stipendiary curate lacking the ability to '*master the evils which here surround him*'. The result was '*moral and spiritual pollution almost as great as the physical*'. Fletcher concluded his report with a consideration of the physical condition of the weavers in the area. He noted inferior physical characteristics such as reduced stature and muscular deficiency, as well as widespread ill-health that included a high rate of tuberculosis of the neck (scrofula). Fletcher also referred to extensive mental ill-health within the community which ranged from anxiety to insanity, no doubt caused by fluctuations, sometimes very severe, in the silk trade.

Fletcher's overall assessment of the state of weavers in Nuneaton as a consequence of the collapse in the silk trade when prohibition ended was hard-hitting:

> *In the neighbourhoods of Nuneaton, Bulkington and Foleshill, the usual condition of a number of journeyhand families is that of the greatest dirt and misery, sometimes with no bedsteads but beds of wrappers, stuffed with straw, and without any linen to them. Sometimes the bed consists merely of chaff held together with bricks, and covered with a wrapper. Their food in these instances consists mainly of bread and butter, potatoes, and a little tea, with occasionally a few poor scraps of bacon. This class are commonly in extreme*

63   Ibid., p. 71–2.
64   Searby, p. 108–9.
65   Fletcher, p. 75.

PUBLIC HEALTH ACT,

(11 & 12 Vict., Cap. 63.)

REPORT

TO THE

GENERAL BOARD OF HEALTH,

ON A

PRELIMINARY INQUIRY

INTO THE SEWERAGE, DRAINAGE, AND SUPPLY OF
WATER, AND THE SANITARY CONDITION
OF THE INHABITANTS

OF THE PARISHES OF

NUNEATON AND CHILVERS COTON.

BY GEORGE THOMAS CLARK,

SUPERINTENDING INSPECTOR.

LONDON:
PRINTED BY W. CLOWES & SONS, STAMFORD STREET,
FOR HER MAJESTY'S STATIONERY OFFICE.
1849.

distress...their condition far worse than an agricultural labourer. Rudeness and misery seem to be the inevitable condition of the mere journeyhand in the single-hand trade. These almost everywhere exhibit an appearance of wretchedness. The whole appearance of single-hand districts, and of their inhabitants, is one of rudeness, poverty and depression.[66]

The consequences for the state of public health in Nuneaton around this time were made clear in a *General Board of Health Report on Nuneaton and Chilvers Coton* published in 1849, some 17 years after Polly Button's murder. It would seem that little, if anything, had been done to stem the tide of death and disease amongst the town's poor that arose directly from the insanitary conditions that were prevalent in the town in Polly Button's lifetime. The town's first ever cholera outbreak had begun just a few months after her murder, in September 1832, and spread rapidly due to the appalling state of the cramped courts along Abbey Street in which Polly Button and a large proportion of the town's population lived. Indeed, more than half of those who died in the cholera outbreak were residents of Abbey Street. The mortality rate in Nuneaton is likely to have been in excess of 30 per 1,000 in the years around 1832. With the Census Commissioners estimating the national average mortality rate in 1831 to have been 18.5 per 1,000[67], Nuneaton's death rate at this time greatly exceeded the national average. To provide some indication of the health risk associated with this rate of mortality, one can refer to William Farr, the leading British epidemiologist of the time who was a pioneer in the field of medical statistics in the nineteenth century. Farr had written: '*A sustained rate of mortality above 17 in 1,000 always implies*

---

66   Fletcher, p. 302.

67   Woods & Woodward, p. 21.

unfavourable sanitary conditions; …any rate above 30 implies **sanitary conditions highly destructive to human life**'[68] (my emphasis). That Polly Button successfully raised all her five children in the squalor and filth of such a shocking and damaging environment must be recognised as a significant maternal achievement.

The author of the Public Health report, George Thomas Clark, gave specific attention to the courts of Abbey Street, describing them as '*seats of fever and smallpox… ill-paved, damp, undrained and in a very filthy and offensive condition*',[69] a description he felt could be applied to most of the rest of the town. He quantified the main sources of nuisance and disease as comprising a total of more than a thousand pigsties, privies, cesspools and slaughterhouses. The lack of an adequate and properly laid piped sewerage system for the town, combined with extensive use by the inhabitants of wells that may sometimes have been as shallow as only nine feet deep, posed a grave threat to people's health. Clark's summary on his findings was quite scathing: '*Public nuisances consist of open dung-heaps, stagnant and foul pools and ditches, unmade or ill-made roads, privies having no drain and exposed to highways. The present state of the town I found to be the subject of universal complaint. The darkness adds materially to the labours of the police and promotes gross immoralities. These, the darkness itself and the dirty condition of the public ways combine to render Nuneaton a place through which a respectable female could not safely walk after nightfall.*'[70]

For a final comment in this chapter on the state of Nuneaton around this time, one could do worse than look to its most famous daughter, the novelist George Eliot. In the story *Janet's Repentance* in *Scenes of Clerical Life*, set in Milby (Nuneaton) in the 1830s, Eliot makes a stark reference to '*the pallid sufferers up dim entries, languishing under the tardy death of want and misery.*'

We now have a clear understanding of the important, if not critical, background factors that give insight into the couple's desperate situation. The telling of the story of Polly Button's murder can now move on to the foul and fatal deed itself.

---

68 Humphreys, p. 121.
69 Clark, para. 18.
70 Clark, para. 51.

DARKNESS ON THE
EDGE OF TOWN

Murder Most Foul

First Written Account of the Murder

The place where Polly Button was attacked by John Danks on the evening of Saturday 18 February 1832 lay in a quiet location on the very outskirts of Nuneaton (see Figure 11). Danks's deadly assault took place in an open-sided barn, known locally at the time as 'Astley's hovel'. The nearest roadway was Occupation Road, now known as Aston Road, which ran from Abbey Green, at the top of Abbey Street, towards a path that led onwards to Weddington Meadows. The first written record of her murder was made by the local diarist John Astley (see Figure 15), in an entry in his diary erroneously recorded as Sunday 20 February [the Sunday would have been the 19th]. The entry must have been made in retrospect some days later, as Astley refers to events that happened after the Sunday in question.

Astley recorded that:

A whoman named Green commonly called Polly Button was found this morning lying in the road in a field occupied by Mr Beasley leading from Mr Astley's New Mill Field Barn with her throat horribly cut and was Dead. It was not doubted but that the whoman was murdered, the situation when found was ab't 22 yds from Mr

Fig. 15. John Astley's
Nuneaton Diary entry
for 'Sunday Feb 20',
containing the first
written record
of the murder of
Polly Button.

Astley's hovel where it was evident the bloody deed was committed wholly or in part from the large quantity of Blood found to be on the Straw therein and on the Gate of the Field in wh. the Hovel was in. Groups of people contin'd to visit the Body/ the spot on this and several succeeding days. Suspicion fell upon a Farmers Labouring Carpenter of the name of John Danks who was immediately taken into custody. On Tuesday an Inquest was held on the body before Seymour, Esq. (Coroner) which was not concluded and was adjourned 'till the following day when the Jury returned a verdict of willful murder against the Prisoner John Danks who in the course of the evening made a confession in confidence to the Rev'd. Mr. King, Curate of NEaton.

INQUEST INTO THE DEATH OF MARY GREEN

Local newspapers were quick to follow up with reports of the dramatic events surrounding the murder of Polly Button – from the finding of the body in the roadway near Astley's hovel to the arrest of the principal suspect, John Danks, and the ensuing inquest held at The Britannia public house in Abbey Street, Nuneaton, from 21–22 February 1832. Local newspapers featuring the story prominently included the *Coventry Herald* (24 February) and the *Leamington Spa Courier* (25 February). News of the murder was also reported in many other parts of the country, most likely through the rapid syndication of news about such notorious events. For the first time, people in the area were able to gain an insight into the background of Polly Button and John Danks's stormy affair and the sequence of events that had taken place on the evening of the murder and after Polly Button's body had been discovered in the early hours of the following morning. The summary that follows is derived from the *Coventry*

Herald's report on 24 February 1832. A full transcript of the newspaper's report is given in Annexe 3.

The newspaper announced the '*perpetration of an appalling murder of an unfortunate and wretched woman*' named Mary Green, otherwise better known by the name of Polly Button. The report stated that she had been a single woman, living with her five illegitimate children in a small house at the top of Abbey Street, Nuneaton. Polly Button was described as being about forty years of age, of low stature, and of a '*disagreeable appearance*'. The article gave details of her three-year relationship with a married man called John Danks, who had fathered one child and against whom Polly Button had recently affiliated another child, due to be born within a few weeks. Animosity was known to exist between Polly Button and Danks's wife, with quarrels ensuing between the three of them.

The newspaper report went on to describe the events that appeared to have taken place on the night of the murder, with Danks calling on Polly Button and the couple going out for a walk across a field at the rear of the house towards Astley's hovel. Polly Button did not return home that evening and nothing was heard of her until early the following morning, Sunday 19 February, when her blood-soaked body was found near the hovel.

The parish constable, Joseph Haddon, had arrested Danks on Nuneaton Common, now part of present-day Stockingford, shortly afterwards on suspicion of murdering Polly Button and taken him to the Red Lion public house in Wash Lane, present-day Queen's Road. Here Danks was searched and some of his clothes were removed for further, closer examination. He was then taken to the nearby gaol, located in what is now Stratford Street, Nuneaton. On the steps to the gaol he acknowledged the growing crowd of people in front of the building by nonchalantly taking off his hat and waving it three or four times above his head.

Several notable gentlemen of the town, including one of the town's solicitors, James Williams Buchanan, had started to seek out information connected with the incident. Some potentially incriminating items had been found in Danks's house which had initially led the investigators to believe that Danks's wife was also concerned with the murder, although she vehemently denied all participation in the foul deed. She did, however, acknowledge that on Sunday morning when in bed with her husband, he had said to her, '*Well, Polly Button will never disturb another family, for I cut her head almost off, and threw the knife into the hedge.*' This admission was to aid the discovery, on the Tuesday following the murder, of a blood-covered pocketknife later identified as belonging to Danks.

At 10am on Tuesday 21 February, an inquest into the death of Polly Button was opened at The Britannia public house. Danks was described as being '*about five feet four inches in height, between 40 and 50 years of age, by trade a carpenter, and by no means of a forbidding countenance, nor was there anything in his appearance indicative of a mind capable of committing the crime with which he stood charged*'. The examination of witnesses lasted until four o'clock that afternoon, when an adjournment took place until the following day. After a further two hours of hearing evidence on the Wednesday morning, Danks was brought into the room shackled in irons and placed before the coroner for the purpose of having the evidence read out to him and to call any witnesses. Afterwards, the room was cleared for the jury to consider its verdict. Danks did not have to wait very long. After a brief period of consultation, the foreman of the jury announced to those in attendance that it had found that Mary Green had been wilfully murdered, and that John Danks had been the person who committed the murder.

On the short journey back to the gaol, Danks was followed by a large crowd who expressed their feelings towards him through a continual barrage of groans and hisses. There being no evidence against his wife, Jane, she had been ordered to be set free. It was reported that she had seemed extremely emotional, perhaps deranged to some extent. Later that day she had evaded the person charged with looking after her in Constable Haddon's house and had run furiously up Abbey Street, hidden in a temporarily unoccupied house, and locked the door behind her. When, eventually, her hiding place had been found, the door had to be forced open and she had been found cowering in terror in a corner of an upstairs room.

Danks travelled to Warwick on Thursday 23 February, the day after the inquest verdict had been announced and the same day that Polly Button was buried in the local parish church. He was escorted to Warwick gaol by Constable Haddon and it was during this journey that a conversation took place between them that brought up a significant issue of admissibility of evidence in the trial that was to follow in just over five weeks' time. At Warwick gaol, Danks would have spent his time in one of the austere cells (Figure 16), no doubt contemplating his predicament with increasing dread.

Fig. 16. Cell at Warwick Gaol, from Marden's *The Murder of Polly Button*.

THE PRICE YOU PAY

The Trial, Execution and Dissection of John Danks

The Trial – Background and Commencement

Due to the nature of the offence and the severity of the potential penalty of death on conviction, the trial of John Danks was held at the Warwickshire spring assizes at Warwick Crown Court, Northgate Street, Warwick, commencing at 8am on Friday, 30 March 1832. It was to last more than six hours.[71]

The Warwick Crown Court building survives (Figure 17), as do the cells in which prisoners were kept awaiting trial. Figure 18 shows the corridor from the cells, at the far end of which is the small and narrow staircase that leads up directly into the prisoners' dock in the courtroom. Danks would have trudged this route before coming up to appear before the court. The view Danks would have had when he entered the prisoners' dock is shown in Figure 22.

The case was heard over the course of that day in front of the Midland Circuit judge, Justice James Parke, the legal representatives

---

71 Blomly.

Left: **Fig. 17.** Warwick Crown Court, Northgate Street, Warwick.

Right: **Fig. 18.** Corridor leading from the prisoners' cells to the courtroom, Warwick Crown Court.

being Serjeant-at-Law John Adams and Mr Andrew Amos (prosecuting), and Messrs Clarke and Daniels (defence). A press report at the time indicated that the spring assizes at Warwick had been the heaviest that had occurred for many years.[72] The Warwickshire spring assizes were the last in the series on the Midland Circuit (comprising Northamptonshire, Rutland, Lincolnshire, Nottinghamshire, Derbyshire, Leicestershire and Warwickshire) for Justice Parke, who had been engaged in a busy schedule hearing cases since 27 February. He had arrived in Warwick, from Coventry, in the early hours of Sunday, 25 March 1832 and had begun hearing cases early the following morning. Due to the large number of cases to be tried at Warwick, Justice Parke was to sit from eight o'clock in the morning until half past ten at night on at least one occasion.

One newspaper reported an early address by Mr Justice Parke to a jury, when he had said, '*That he looked forward with very painful feelings to the duties which he as Judge, and they as Jurymen,*

72 *Coventry Herald*, 30 March 1832.

had to perform. It was not because the cases were extremely numerous, although there were not less than one hundred and fifty prisoners for trial (a great number, considering that the Magistrates had recently held a General Sessions, at which they had disposed of about one hundred more) but because the calendar appeared to contain an instance of almost every species of crime, not only of fraud, but of violence, and bloodshed, and of almost every offence depraved human nature was capable of committing.'[73]

The judge and both prosecuting counsel at the trial had interesting and noteworthy lives.

JUSTICE JAMES PARKE (1782–1868) (FIGURE 19)

On 22 March 1832, just over a week before the trial, Justice James Parke had turned fifty years of age. As a young man he had attended Trinity College, Cambridge, where he had established himself as a brilliant legal academic, winning several scholarships and awards. He had been called to the bar at the Inner Temple in 1813. On 28 November 1828, Parke was appointed a Justice of the Court of King's Bench and was also subsequently knighted on 1 December of the same year. He was created Baron Wensleydale in 1856. As a trial judge, it was recorded that Parke was grave but not pompous, and that he was patient and courteous. He apparently had a passion for fresh air, insisting that windows should be open even on the coldest day; so, at one assize *'the jury, each member with a different colour handkerchief over his head, a shivering sheriff, and despairing Ordinary, presented a sufficiently comical scene to those not too frozen to be amused at it.'*[74] We don't know whether Parke had insisted on open windows at Danks's trial in March 1832!

Fig. 19.
Justice James Parke, judge at the trial of John Danks.
©National Portrait Gallery, London.

73 *Northampton Mercury*, 7 April 1832.
74 Jones.

Above: **Fig. 20.**
John Adams,
prosecuting counsel
at the trial of
John Danks.

Below: **Fig. 21.**
Andrew Amos,
prosecuting counsel
at the trial of John
Danks.

JOHN ADAMS (1786–1856) (FIGURE 20)

John Adams was born in 1786, the third son of Simon Adams, Esq., of Ansty Hall, near Coventry. He had adopted the legal profession early in life and practised with marked success on the Midland Circuit, attaining the rank of Serjeant-at-Law. In press reports of Danks's trial he was referred to as Serjeant Adams. He was later described as *'eccentric and somewhat rough and abrupt in his manner, although possessed of much knowledge and sound sense.'*[75] Just four years after the trial, in June 1836, Adams and five other lawyers met in Lincoln's Inn Fields and founded the New Law Life Assurance Society, which would eventually become Legal and General. Adams was elected its first chairman, a position he held until 1856. The photograph in Figure 20 was taken from a portrait of Adams at Legal and General's head office in London.

ANDREW AMOS (1791–1860) (FIGURE 21)

Amos was born in 1791 in India, was educated at Eton and graduated from Trinity College, Cambridge in 1813. He was called to the bar by the Middle Temple and joined the Midland Circuit, which included Warwickshire. Amos had been appointed the first professor of English Law at London University, now called University College London, upon its establishment in 1826, and in the following years his lectures achieved celebrity and popularity, being attended sometimes by up to as many as

---

75   Walford, pp. 135–136.

150 students. The circumstances of the murder of Polly Button were to feature in these lectures and form the basis of articles in both medical journals and major medico-legal textbooks. In 1848, he was elected Downing Professor of the Laws of England at Cambridge University, an office he held till his death on 18 April 1860. It was from his portrait at the University of Cambridge law library that the photograph (Figure 21) has been taken for this publication.

Unfortunately, the records of trials on the Midland Circuit were destroyed by a clerk later in the nineteenth century and do not exist for trials earlier than 1860. As a consequence, the only sources we have for establishing what happened in court during the trial are the newspaper reports of the time, which, in the main, comprise the *Leamington Spa Courier* and the *Warwick and Warwickshire Advertiser* (both 31 March 1832), and the *Coventry Herald* and the *Leicester Journal* (both 6 April 1832). These reports did not record the questions raised by either the prosecuting or defence counsel, or the judge, merely the answers that were given by the witnesses in response to such questioning. At times, therefore, a degree of analysis and interpretation has been necessary to provide a meaningful and reasoned account of the testimony that was given in court.

Several people from Nuneaton had set out in gigs and carriages at approximately 3.30am on the day of the trial for the journey to Warwick, via Coventry, to attend the Crown Court. The travel arrangements for the group, comprising mainly witnesses who had been called to appear, were as follows:[76]

Haddon's cart: Elizabeth Green (daughter, eyewitness), James Green (nephew, eyewitness), William Wagstaff (finder of the murder weapon), George Hawkins (called to give evidence relating to Danks and the murder weapon), Joseph Lakin, Ralph Thomas, George Morris (the latter called to give evidence relating to Danks and ownership of the murder weapon), John and Thomas Bates (called to give evidence relating to Danks's explanation of blood being found on his clothing).

---

76 Warwickshire County Record Office, The Examination of John Danks DR280/56/98A.

Barraclough's cart: Sarah Hammond (resident of Abbey Street, heard Polly Button's cries for help), Richard Harris (neighbour of Hammond, went to investigate the cries for help), John Aston (lodger at Danks's house).

Mr Warner's gig: John Warner, Richard Lloyd (surgeon in Nuneaton, examined Polly Button's dead body).

Mr Beasley's gig: Richard Beasley (first to find the body, owner/occupier of land where the body was found), Thomas Lees (land surveyor, drew the map used at the trial).

The trial began with the empanelling of the twelve-man jury. The press reported that Danks was charged with the wilful murder of Mary Green, alias Polly Button, at Nuneaton on 21 February 1832. It seems that inaccuracy in press reporting has been a long-standing problem, given that Polly Button was actually murdered on 18 February! Danks entered a plea of not guilty, as he had done earlier at the coroner's inquest in Nuneaton. Court reporters saw Danks as a mild, inoffensive-looking man who appeared somewhat dazed and perhaps not fully aware of what was going on around him. Some reported him appearing to look anxiously around the courtroom, perhaps seeking the familiarity of some expected acquaintances. Figure 22 represents the view that Danks would have had when he first appeared in the prisoners' dock at Warwick Crown Court, with the positions of the judge, counsel, jury, witness stand, press and public gallery as shown.

Fig. 22. Danks's view from the prisoners' dock, Court Room 1, Warwick Crown Court, showing positions of interested parties.

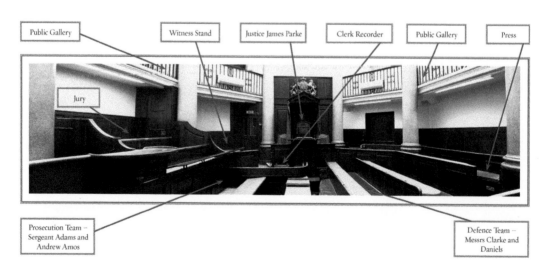

| Public Gallery | Witness Stand | Justice James Parke | Clerk Recorder | Public Gallery | Press |

Jury

Prosecution Team –
Sergeant Adams and
Andrew Amos

Defence Team –
Messrs Clarke and
Daniels

Evidence Presented at the Trial

SEQUENCE OF EVENTS ON THE NIGHT OF THE MURDER

The events of the fateful night in question were established primarily from the evidence of a small number of key witnesses: Elizabeth Green, Polly's 17-year-old daughter; James Green, Polly's nephew, aged 22 and a stocking weaver by trade; Sarah Hammond, aged about 63, a resident of Abbey Street; Richard Harris, who was Hammond's next door neighbour; and John Aston, a lodger at the Danks's family home.

John Danks lived just a few houses away from Polly Button in Upper Abbey Street ('*at the top of Abbey-End*'). A new georeferenced map commissioned for this publication gives a distance of nearly 80 metres between the two houses.[77] Danks used to call on her, rapping on the window of her house when he arrived for her to come out and go for a walk. Sometimes this may have been a relatively short walk to Astley's hovel, a place that offered them some privacy or, indeed, intimacy. Longer walks would appear to have also been taken to Weddington Meadows, along a scenic route that led to the banks of the River Anker. Evidence for this is derived both from a contemporary reference of the time (*The Ghost Walk of Weddington*, a play about the murder of Polly Button) and references to Weddington passed on in the oral tradition by local inhabitants over the years. Such walks, leading from the top of Abbey Street to Weddington, would most likely have been enhanced by the opening of the Weddington Meadows bridge across the River Anker on 2 January 1818, paid for by Lionel Place of Weddington Castle.[78] Figure 23 shows the first Ordnance Survey map covering Nuneaton (1835), with the location of Astley's hovel and Polly Button's house shown in relation to Weddington.

At the trial, both Elizabeth and James bore witness to the fact that on previous occasions they had seen Polly Button and Danks walk out together over the burgage fields to the location they called Astley's hovel, a hovel being the term used at the time for

---

77   SCG Cartography and Design – email correspondence, 2 March 2018.
78   Brookes.

Above: **Fig. 23.** 1835 Ordnance Survey Map showing the location of Astley's hovel and Polly Button's House.

Below: **Fig. 24.** Illustration of Astley's hovel in Marden's *The Murder of Polly Button.*

an open-sided building used for sheltering cattle (Figure 24). James had stated that he knew Astley's hovel well and that on at least two former occasions he had seen Danks and his aunt go there by night.

Piecing together a clear and definite sequence of events and timings for Danks calling at Polly Button's house on the evening of Saturday 18 February presents some difficulties, given the summarised nature of the responses by James and Elizabeth to questions recorded in the press reports. Some of the responses seem to be contradictory, for example Elizabeth stating that Danks had arrived just after 8pm whereas James said that he had arrived at 7pm or just after. Given statements of timings by James and two other witnesses that indicate the earlier timing is the more likely or consistent, the assumption has been made that either Elizabeth gave the 8pm time in error or it was misreported in the press.

From a close review of the testimony of all witnesses, it would seem that the following is the most likely sequence of events at Polly Button's house on the night of the murder. Danks had knocked on the door or window of Polly Button's house at some time between 7.00–7.15pm. He had then opened the door and said, '*Mary, come here, I want to speak to you*'. Elizabeth confirmed to the court that Danks had spoken in his usual way. Polly had put down Jane, her two-year-old daughter by Danks, and gone out to talk to him, shutting the door behind her. From behind a curtain inside the house

Elizabeth had then watched the couple standing and talking in the yard. James had arrived at his aunt's house at this point and noticed Polly and Danks talking in the yard. James had continued on into the house and Polly, having seen her nephew go inside, promptly followed him inside too. We can only assume that Polly and Danks had been discussing the need to go out that evening, most likely to discuss the forthcoming birth and the issue of maintenance for the child that had arisen following the recent involvement of the Poor Law guardians. Perhaps aware that her children were hungry, Polly gave priority to attending to their needs and went out with her daughter to buy two loaves of bread from a nearby bakery, such a sparse meal confirming the family's very limited means. They were gone for about ten minutes or so, leaving James alone in the house with Polly's remaining four children: William, aged 14; Hannah, aged 11; Ann, aged 5; and Jane, aged 2. While both Polly and Elizabeth were out, James had heard something tap or rattle against the window. He had gone outside and noticed Danks standing in the burgage field at the back, behind the courtyard's three-feet high perimeter wall and against the privy, their small outhouse containing the communal toilet for the court. He had crossed the yard, a distance of about ten yards from the door, and asked Danks what he was doing there, to which he received no reply. James had then gone back into the house. Perhaps Danks had been trying to give Polly an agreed signal to indicate that he was ready – perhaps even keen – to go on their walk that evening? Shortly after this incident, Polly and Elizabeth had returned home with the family's meagre meal.

The weather conditions and visibility on the night of the murder were raised as issues in court. The newspaper reports again show that Elizabeth and James had slightly different recollections. Elizabeth had said, '*It was dark but rather starlight; it was a foggy night and dark; I did see some stars that night*', whereas James had recalled the night being '*a star-light night; a fine night; no clouds about that I saw*'. The National Meteorological Library and Archive have confirmed that February 1832 was exceptionally dry.[79] Although

---

79   Joan Self, Archive Information Officer, NMLA – email correspondence, 19 May 2017.

there are few weather records surviving from that time, there is one diary from the Midlands that contains specific measurements that show February 1832 had in fact been one of the driest months of the entire year, with a total of just 1.06 inches of rain on only four days in the month when it had fallen. In addition, a full moon was recorded on Thursday 16 February, just two days before the murder. It would therefore seem that the testimony given by James of good visibility on the night of the murder is more likely to be correct.

James and Elizabeth decided to go into town that evening. After Elizabeth had put on her bonnet, they both left the house and walked the few yards across the courtyard into the entry that led to Abbey Street. They remained chatting in the entry for about ten to fifteen minutes. In due course, they saw Polly emerge from the house, lock the door behind her, put the key in her pocket and then walk to the rainwater cistern at the rear of the courtyard. At this point James had then left Elizabeth briefly and moved from the entry back into the yard, from where he had observed his aunt and Danks at the rear perimeter wall. James saw Polly climb upon the cistern and be helped over the wall into the burgage field by Danks and then watched them walk a dozen or so yards in the direction of Astley's hovel. Elizabeth confirmed that that there had been no way for her mother to get out of the yard in that direction except by getting over the wall and into the burgage field beyond. James was almost certain that Danks would have known that he had seen them go off together and be aware of the direction in which they had headed. James put the time that they got over the wall as about 7.30pm. James and Elizabeth had then gone into town together, probably attracted by the fact that the town's market was still taking place, as it typically ran until nine or ten o'clock on Saturday nights.

Elizabeth had returned home sometime between ten and eleven o'clock that evening but found the door locked. She had spent the next hour or so going to several neighbours' houses trying to find her mother but to no avail. She returned home and was let in through the window by her brother, William. She had sat up all night, with mounting concern as to what may have happened to her mother. Joseph Haddon, the constable, had then called at their house early on the Sunday morning to tell her the awful news that her mother had been found murdered. As much as Haddon tried to obtain information from Elizabeth as to what may have happened, she was unable to respond at all owing to her profound distress.

TWO WITNESSES WHO HEARD POLLY'S CRIES OF DISTRESS

Sarah Hammond was in her early 60s and lived alone in her own house, adjacent to a garden belonging to a Mr Tingle and overlooking the burgage fields at the back of the Half Moon Inn in Abbey Street. Mrs Hammond gave evidence that she thought the distance between her house and the hovel was about 500 yards. The actual distance to the centre of the barn, where the couple most probably had their argument and where Danks launched his fatal attack, in fact has been calculated to be 634 yards.[80] Hammond told the court that she had been at home on the night of the murder and had been sitting in a room, the window of which faced the burgage field. She had heard '*the dreadful cry of a woman*' and, on opening her door, had heard further cries of '*Oh, Oh! Loose me, loose me!*'. Hammond thought that the cries had come from somewhere nearby in the direction of the burgage fields but could not confirm to the court from what particular part they had originated. She had then heard afterwards some groans and a cry of '*Oh, oh!*', whereupon she had knocked on the window of her next-door neighbour, Richard Harris. She had told him of the cries, and her opinion that there was '*a man pulling a girl about*'.

Harris told the court that he had heard nothing until that time and came out to listen. He made out the cry of '*Oh! Oh!*' two or three times over. On hearing this, he went to locate the source of the sounds. He went through the door leading out of the yard into the burgage fields and walked fifty or sixty yards in the direction of the cries. However, the cries having ceased and it then being quiet he decided to turn back, acknowledging that he had not gone as far as he thought the cries had come from. Harris stated that it was as near light as it possibly could be, perhaps meaning that although

---

80   Stuart Gill of SCG Cartography, email correspondence (23 May 2017).

it was night-time, there was sufficient moonlight to see well enough. In his evidence to the court, Harris said that he believed the cries were from a person who seemed to have been in violent distress and appeared to him to have come from a place closer than Astley's hovel. He stated that he didn't think the cries had been a quarter of a mile off. This issue was picked up by both the judge and the defence team, as they spent some time questioning both Harris and Hammond about the weather and any prevailing wind direction on the evening in question. Hammond couldn't be sure if it had been a windy night or not, and neither could he recall the direction of any wind. Research has confirmed that the wind came from a northward direction on a majority of days in February.[81] With Astley's hovel lying to the north-northwest of Hammond's house, the weather being very dry and with temperatures above freezing, these factors may account for the significant distance Polly's cries for help actually travelled that night.

The fact that Polly Button's cries of distress seem to have gone on for sufficient time for Harris to be called out by his neighbour and for him to then hear them across the burgage fields suggests that the argument in the hovel had got progressively worse rather than Danks launching an unexpected and debilitating violent attack. It may be the case that their argument descended into an increasingly physical struggle, with the couple grappling in anger until it got to the point where Danks violently lashed out, first with his fist, and then with his knife, *'in order to stop her hooting'*.

WHAT THE LODGER SAW

Not much actually! John Aston had been a lodger at the Danks's home in Abbey Street for five months before the evening of the murder. There were no other lodgers and no children in the household. In evidence to the court, Aston recalled that Danks and his wife, Jane, had gone out a little before seven o'clock on the Saturday evening and Jane had returned on her own, carrying a pair of stockings, no more than half an hour later. Aston was

---

81   Joan Self, Archive Information Officer, National Meteorological Library
     and Archive, email correspondence 19 May 2017.

not feeling very well that night, so he had gone to bed about ten minutes after Jane had come back and had gone to sleep quickly. He had not seen anything further of John Danks after the couple had left the house earlier that evening.

FINDING THE BODY

Richard Beasley was a draper living in Abbey Street and had been resident in the town for forty years. He occupied a number of fields to the north of Abbey Street, including Barn Close pasture (the field that contained Astley's hovel). Beasley acknowledged the area as being '*a place of resort of men and women, as in all places of large population*'. He and his manservant had gone to the site between six and seven o'clock on the morning of Sunday 19 February. This would have been just prior to dawn breaking, sunrise being at quarter past seven on that day. In the early morning gloom, their lamps would have been throwing light onto the track ahead. He told the court that they had noticed something in the road and when they reached it, they had found a lifeless body lying about fifteen yards from the hovel, face downward and with a great deal of blood by it. Beasley had gone to the nearest house for assistance, probably one of a small run of properties in Occupation Road (now Aston Road) near Abbey Green. In the meantime, his manservant went back towards the town to find the parish constable, Joseph Haddon. Beasley informed the court that he hadn't seen any murder weapon lying near the body.

ENTER CONSTABLE HADDON

Appointed as the constable of Nuneaton in 1810 when aged about 30, Joseph Haddon's typical workload of dealing with Nuneaton's problems of drunkenness, social disorder, fighting and theft was to change dramatically in the early morning of Sunday 19 February when he was called on by Beasley's manservant. The manservant quickly told Haddon what had just been discovered and they had both gone immediately to Astley's hovel. On approaching the hovel, Haddon had seen the dead body of a woman lying face downward in the middle of the roadway with her head towards Nuneaton's town centre. Haddon described the body position as being very straight, with the right arm very nearly under the body and the left arm by the side. The face of the person had been obscured by a blood-soaked cap that was stuck to the skin, but when Haddon had peeled this back, he had immediately identified the body as being that of Mary Green. Haddon had subsequently searched the area near where the body had been found and noted that there was a great deal of blood on both sides of a gate that gave access to Astley's hovel, and the mark of a person's right hand on the gate. The trail of blood continued from the gate to the hovel, which he described as being open at one end and enclosed at the other. Inside the hovel he observed that there was a good deal of blood on the straw on the floor and that there was cow dung present. He had been unable to find any sharp instrument or knife nearby.

Newspaper reports quote Haddon as stating that he had attended the murder scene with the surgeon, Mr John Bond. Haddon had sent to the workhouse for a blanket to cover the body and arranged for a door to be used to carry Polly Button's body back to her house in Upper Abbey Street, arriving there sometime after eight o'clock that morning. Subsequently, Haddon had then sought out another surgeon, Richard Lloyd, to examine the body at Polly Button's house and to assist him in investigating the murder. Haddon was probably aware of Lloyd's significant experience of lacerating wounds from his time as a surgeon in the army. It was clear to all that the throat had been cut, accounting for the great deal of blood that had been seen on the body and near where the body lay. After the examination of the body, Haddon had gone back to conduct a careful search of the area around the crime scene but had still not been able to find the murder weapon.

Given the well-known turbulent relationship between Danks, his wife and Polly Button, either Haddon was already aware of the potential for Danks's involvement in the murder or someone in the locality may have suggested Danks as a suspect. The time was still quite early and Haddon decided to go to Danks's home just a few houses away from Polly Button's house along Abbey Street towards the town centre. Danks was not at home, but Haddon still undertook a search of the property. Afterwards, Haddon continued to search for Danks and within the hour had found him about a mile and a half away on Nuneaton Common (now Stockingford) walking towards Nuneaton. Danks had later told Haddon that he had been to get some money from his master and was on his way back home when Haddon had taken him into custody. Haddon had then taken Danks to the Red Lion public house in Wash Lane (present-day Queens Road), the time being about nine o'clock in the morning.

CONSTABLE HADDON'S EVIDENCE AGAINST DANKS

Blood: Haddon described to the court how there had been a great deal of blood at the scene: near the body, lying about the gate on both sides, between the gate and the hovel, along the side of the hovel, and inside the hovel, including on the straw and cow dung within. A later commentary on the trial confirmed that evidence had been presented of bloody marks from both of Polly Button's hands on the gate, while Danks's hand was also marked on the gate, but at a different place.[82]

He then went on to describe items of clothing that he had identified as being connected with the prisoner. The first of these had been a cloth button. When Haddon searched Danks at the Red Lion public house, he got him to remove the two waistcoats he was wearing so that he could examine their buttons more specifically. Having confirmed that he had not found any other waistcoat when he had searched Danks's home, Haddon continued, saying that he had seen a button or two on one of the waistcoats which he thought had been sewn on recently. At this point in the trial, one of these waistcoats, a red flush one, was produced and shown to the jury and it was observed that there were some buttons that did not match with the rest. Haddon told the court that he had found a button near the gate that led to Astley's hovel which corresponded with others on the waistcoat and on which was a small spot of blood. He informed the court that as the gate had been locked, he surmised that Danks must have needed to climb over it to go from the hovel and that by implication the button had become detached at this location. Haddon had placed the button in a piece of paper,

---

82   Taylor, p. 442.

retained it in his pocket and had presented it before the coroner at the inquest that had followed in Nuneaton. He told the court that the bloodspot had been a little visible when it had been shown to the coroner but that it had since worn off.

The court turned its attention to further items of Danks's clothing that had been found to be spotted with blood – a pair of trousers and some stockings. Haddon said that he had gone from the Red Lion public house, where Danks was being held initially, to fetch a pair of spare trousers from Danks's house. On his return some ten minutes later, and Danks having removed his trousers so he could examine them more closely, Haddon noticed there were some small spots of blood on them. The trousers were shown to the court in confirmation of Haddon's evidence. Haddon had also noticed that Danks was wearing a clean pair of stockings. As a consequence of this observation, after Danks had been taken to the guardhouse in Stratford Street, Haddon went back to Danks's house and undertook a further search. He found a pair of dirty black stockings, on one of which was a spot of blood. At this point, the stockings were also produced for the court to examine.

Mr James Williams Buchanan, a solicitor from Nuneaton and a member of the prosecution team, also gave evidence at the trial. He confirmed that he had been present when the prisoner had been examined before the coroner at the inquest in Nuneaton. At the inquest, Danks's examination had been taken down in writing and read back to him. Danks had been cautioned not to say anything but had proceeded to refer to the presence of blood on his trousers: '*Mr Haddon says there are some spots of blood upon my breeches, and there might be, for I was kicked all over, with blood from Mr Place's pig.* [This would have been Mr Lionel Place, Esq., of Weddington Castle]. *John Bates was killing it, and the blood came all over my breeches, my waistcoat, and my face, and I was holding it, and a time before when John Bates' father was killing a pig, I was served in the same way. I have nothing further to say.*' The court then called John Bates and his father, Thomas Bates, as witnesses, who both testified that they had killed some pigs for Mr Place but that Danks had not been near. Buchanan confirmed that Danks had said at the inquest, in his defence, that he had nothing further to say other than that Mr Haddon had spoken wrongly.

Danks's defence team did summon a witness in an attempt to explain how the trousers may have got blood on them. William Cave had been helping Danks work on a gate-post about two weeks before the murder on land between Weddington and Nuneaton. Danks had struck his speck (a digging tool used for loosening hard ground) in the earth and had been cut near the eye by something that had flown up. Drops of blood from the wound had flowed down his clothing and he had wiped it on his sleeve. Cave said he had known Danks for five years and told the court that he thought he had always seemed a humane and peaceful man.

The Boots: The first evidence derived from Danks's boots was that Haddon had found cow dung between the upper leathers and the soles. He presented the boots as an exhibit to the court and confirmed that they were in the same state as when he had found them. He also presented the shoes Polly Button had been wearing and it was noted that there was cow dung on them too. In describing Astley's hovel to the court earlier in his evidence, Haddon had also confirmed the presence of cow dung in the barn itself.

The second piece of evidence related to a missing nail in the toe area of the sole of the right boot which Haddon had spotted when he had examined the shoes of the prisoner on Monday 20 February following the murder. Haddon had subsequently connected the nail deficiency in the right boot with the pattern of footprints in a wheatfield – probably Joseph Cross's 'Top Burgage' field – near where the body was found. To do that, Haddon had revisited the murder scene with Mr Lloyd, the surgeon, and made a fresh impression of the boot by the side of three of the original footmarks in the field. The particular pattern was confirmed in all three. The boot with the deficient nail was shown to the jury, as were the cement casts of the impressions that Haddon and Lloyd had made on site and which also gave a match due to the missing nail. Haddon had traced the footsteps *'from the draw-rails to the gap at the Old Wheel'*, probably across the 'big burgage' field, but was unable to trace them further because after that there was grass.

The Knife: When Haddon had first searched Danks he had asked him where his knife was, to which Danks answered that he had none but a small one in his pocket that belonged to his wife. Haddon had taken possession of this knife. Danks had been unable, or unwilling, to confirm the whereabouts of his own knife to Haddon and came up with some rather weak responses – that it may have been in the cupboard at home and that also he had been filling some holes in a table with putty on the Saturday afternoon and the knife might have dropped down among the sawdust or chips, or might have been burnt. Haddon had searched Danks's house twice after this conversation on Sunday 19 February and examined the workshop in particular, Danks being known as a carpenter of sorts. Haddon found no knife in the cupboard, nor the workshop, but did notice that there were some chips and sawdust present, and some ashes remaining in the grate. Both were examined but no knife or remains of a knife were found. However, on the following Tuesday morning, 21 February, Haddon had taken possession of a blood-stained knife from a William Wagstaff. The knife was shown to the jury at this stage and it was pointed out that there was some oat chaff on the knife, which Haddon confirmed had been sticking to the knife when he had received it from Wagstaff. Haddon then confirmed again to the court that there had been oat straw in the hovel.

Three men were to give further evidence regarding the knife. First, William Wagstaff who confirmed that he had found the knife on the morning of Tuesday 21 February, about four yards from the hedge in Mr Joseph Cross's (top burgage) field, alongside Occupation Road. When questioned by Justice Parke, he estimated the distance from where he had found the knife to the hovel to be 48 yards. Then George Morris gave evidence, stating that he had worked with Danks previously and remembered borrowing his knife on one occasion about six weeks prior to the inquest, i.e. early January. Morris confirmed that the knife that was being shown to him was, as near as he could recollect, the one he had borrowed from Danks, although he felt unable to swear to that effect, saying that he could have found twenty of the kind at the cutler's in Nuneaton. Nuneaton's only cutler at this time would have been Edmund Wasnidge, of Abbey Street.[83] Finally, George

---

83   West, p. 563.

Hawkins gave evidence, stating that Danks had been working at his master's a year previously and had used a knife of his own to cut his food with and had jocularly remarked to him at the time that his knife would do to pick up peas with. The knife had been a black handled one with a broad point, presumably the same description applying to the knife being exhibited to the court.

An expert at Museums Sheffield has suggested that the knife used to murder Polly Button could have been one similar to those shown in Figure 25.[84] All are from the late eighteenth century and are likely to have still been in use around the time of Polly Button's murder.

Fig. 25.
Pocketknives, late eighteenth century.

The Confession: One part of the trial caused a flurry of legal arguments in court – that relating to the admissibility of an alleged confession by Danks during a conversation with Constable Haddon on the way from Nuneaton to Warwick gaol. On that journey, on 23 February, Haddon told the court that he had asked Danks if he had made a confession to Mr King, Nuneaton's curate. Danks had said that he had, and that he had told King more than he should tell any other man. At this point in the trial Mr Clarke, for the defence, objected and raised a concern about evidence arising from any conversation with, or confession to, Constable Haddon that had taken place immediately after Danks's interview with Mr King. He suggested that the latter might have used some threat or held out some inducement to Danks to confess, for example by telling him that it would be better for his soul. As a consequence, Danks may then have been predisposed in making the statements to Haddon by his previous conversation with Mr King. After a brief adjournment, during which Justice Parke discussed the matter with his learned colleague, Mr Baron Bayley, who was also sitting at the assizes, Parke agreed to admit the evidence from Haddon.

The trial resumed with Haddon giving details of the conversation he had held with Danks on the journey to Warwick

84   Clare Starkie, Curator of Decorative Arts, Sheffield Galleries & Museums Trust. Email correspondence, 22 September 2016.

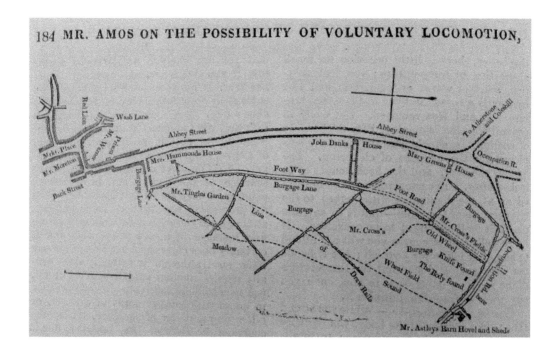

184 MR. AMOS ON THE POSSIBILITY OF VOLUNTARY LOCOMOTION,

Fig. 26.
Map published in
the *London Medical
Gazette* on Saturday
12 May 1832, based
on the trial map drawn
by Thomas Lees.

and which necessitated the examination of a map by the court. To
help the jury familiarise themselves with the layout of Nuneaton
and the principal locations that were being referred to by witnesses,
a map was produced in court that had been drawn by Thomas
Lees, a land surveyor who lived in Abbey Street, Nuneaton. Lees
testified that the situation of the places and delineated distances
on them were correct. In response to a question from the judge,
Lees confirmed that there were some houses between Green's
and Danks's homes. A copy of the map was subsequently used by
Andrew Amos, one of the two prosecuting counsel in the case, in
an article he wrote about the murder and which was published
shortly after the trial in the *London Medical Gazette* (Figure 26).[85]

Haddon had asked Danks specifically if he had '*gone up the
Burgage field, through Joseph Cross's small hand-gate, and through the
top Burgage*'. This approach would have been from Upper Abbey
Street or Abbey End – Abbey Green as it's called now. Danks
replied that he had not gone the way Haddon was suggesting but
had taken a route starting further down Abbey Street, nearer to

85   Amos, pp. 183–6.

the town centre. Danks told Haddon that he had '*gone through Tingle's garden* [Joseph Tingle – variously a maltster, tea dealer, baker, and a resident of Abbey Street] *and over the gap, across the meadow through the green-sward fields to the draw rails; across the wheat field to the gap, where the old wheel lay, and across the old field, into the foot-road, and across the stile to the hovel; to see if the course was clear. Then I turned back to the house of the deceased.*' Given the layout of the town at the time and the fact that a large proportion of the town's inhabitants lived in Abbey Street, in choosing to walk over the burgage fields, meadows and footways to the rear of the houses in Abbey Street, Danks was doing his utmost to avoid drawing attention to himself as he went about his business. This would have been especially important given that the market was still in progress and that people may still have been present in considerable numbers in the town. With his statement to Haddon, Danks's premeditation is clear: whatever his reason for getting Polly Button to come out with him that evening, Danks must have had the possibility of murder on his mind. The extent to which Danks may have been committed in advance to that fatal course of action is, of course, a matter of conjecture.

Figure 27 is a new georeferenced map, derived from the trial map, that more accurately delineates distances between locations. It shows the route taken by Danks, the position of other buildings referred to by witnesses giving evidence in court, and also provides accurately determined locations for the body and the discarded murder weapon.

Danks had then recounted to Haddon how events had unfolded on that Saturday evening. After checking that the coast to the hovel and the hovel itself were clear, he had gone to the rear of the court in which Polly Button lived, threw something at her window and '*called her out*'. She had agreed to this and they had '*walked through the grazing piece, by the foot-road, to Astley's hovel*'. They were in the hovel together about a quarter of an hour. We will never know for sure what they talked about, nor why and when it descended into violence. It would seem likely that the main, if not only, topic of conversation would have been the upcoming birth of their child, due a few weeks later. Polly would have conveyed her very impoverished circumstances and confirmed that the Poor Law guardians were

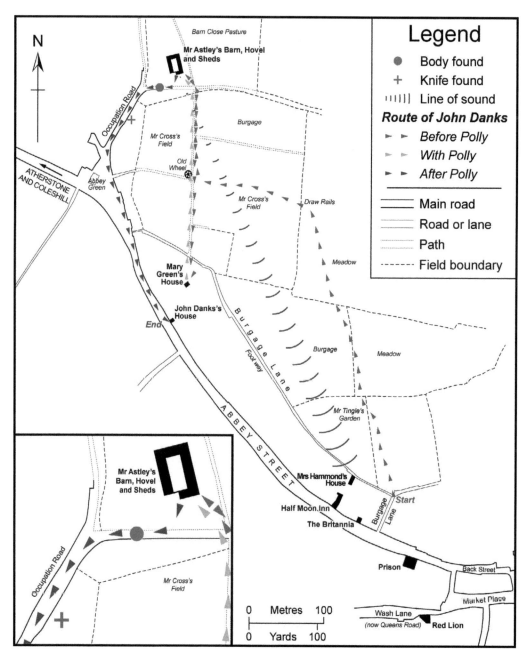

Fig. 27.
A new georeferenced
version of the
trial map.

looking to get Danks to pay maintenance for the child. Danks may also have been told, if he did not know already, that the guardians had found out about the non-payment of the previous maintenance settlement for Jane, his daughter. Danks must have realised the extent of his predicament: the town was in the midst of a savage depression, his limited skills were not sufficient to find secure and settled employment, and carpenters (like many other trades) were struggling to make a living now that the vast majority of the wooden hand-looms in the town were lying idle. Danks's financial position was desperate: he was in considerable debt and had no apparent means to begin settling it. Evidence was given at the trial of animosity existing between Danks's wife, Jane, and Polly Button. We will never know if his wife was aware of the extent of Danks's financial problems, or of his continuing affair with Polly Button, or the fact that Polly Button was pregnant again by her husband. Danks's dilemma would have been two-fold: first, how was he ever going to be able to pay both the outstanding debt in relation to their first child, Jane, and the recently-awarded maintenance payments for what would be his second child with Polly Button, and, second, if his wife didn't know about the debt or the pregnancy, how was he going to find the courage to break the news to her.

Professor Fred Burwick, Research Professor of English at the University of California, Los Angeles, while researching for his 2015 book *British Drama of the Industrial Revolution* came across an original copy of the play *The Ghost Walk of Weddington* in the Mander and Mitchenson collection housed at Old Navy in Greenwich. His summarised account of the text of the play includes a likely motivation for the murder:

> *Not reluctance to give Polly the money due for the child* [due within a few weeks], *but fear of the consequences if his wife found out, kept Danks from paying what was due for his child. Polly and Danks quarrel over money at the tavern, and Danks promises that payment will soon be made.*
>
> [When Polly announces that she is pregnant again] *The Overseers are certain to make a public announcement of his debt. Worse than facing his wife's anger, his arrest is imminent, and he will probably be transported.*

[In the hovel] *Danks begs Polly to wait a bit longer for the money he owes, claiming that he will pay her double as soon as the factory expands. Polly stubbornly objects that she has not enough money to feed her children. Danks grows angry and strikes her, knocking her to the ground.* [86]

Whatever the actual reason and background to their meeting that evening, it would seem that an increasingly heated argument swiftly turned to physical aggression, with Danks grabbing and grappling with Polly Button. This would tally with Mrs Hammond's report of hearing cries of '*Oh, Oh! Loose me, loose me!*' that evening.

Given that Danks had checked that the coast was clear before calling on Polly Button, he must have had in his mind the possibility of murdering her if he could find no other way out of his difficulties. Danks told Haddon that he had raised his fist, struck her on the temple and knocked her to the floor. He had fallen quickly on top of her back and '*cut her once*'. Danks recalled that she had '*hooted very loudly*', so he had '*cut her a second time and stopped her hooting*'. Being '*quite sure she was done for*', Danks had got up, left the hovel, climbed over the locked gate into the adjacent roadway and walked along Occupation Road (now Aston Road) to Abbey Street. Danks said that when he had gone about one hundred yards from the hovel, he thought he had heard the footsteps of a man behind him, so he had spun round but could see no one. He had then shut his knife and thrown it over the hedge into the adjacent wheatfield before making his way to the top of Abbey End and then onwards down Abbey Street to his own house. This would have taken him past the entry to Twitchell's Yard that contained Polly Button's house. Danks told Haddon that on arrival at home he had washed his hands and gone to bed. It would seem that Danks and his wife had then quarrelled about his visits to Polly Button and he had remarked that he would never go with her again and that he had been that night for the last time.[87]

Haddon had asked Danks how it was that he had so little blood on his clothes, considering he had cut Polly Button so

86   Burwick, p. 129.
87   *Leamington Spa Courier*, 7 April 1832.

severely. Danks had replied that when he had knocked her down, he had fallen at her back. Other than his right hand, which was *'very bloody'* – and therefore which must have been the one to hold and wield the knife – he wasn't aware of blood anywhere else.

When asked by the defence counsel Mr Clarke for his opinion of Danks, Haddon had replied that the general character of the prisoner was one of an honest, hard-working man.

A QUESTION OF CHARACTER

One issue that was raised early in proceedings was that of the moral character of Polly Button. Elizabeth, her daughter, confirmed in her evidence that her mother was about six months pregnant, although other accounts at the time indicated that Polly Button may have been just a month away from full term. Although we have only the answers from witnesses and not the questions they were asked in court, from the press reports it would seem that the line of questioning indicated that Polly Button's relations with men were considered to be of some significance. Early press reports, detailed previously, gave particular emphasis to the fact that she was a single mother with five illegitimate children. Syndicated reports in other newspapers characterised her as *'a single woman of loose character'*.[88] Given that the court was attaching importance to Polly Button's possible status as a prostitute – an unfortunately common situation given the deep and widespread poverty of the time – it is perhaps surprising that only one newspaper seems to have used such an unequivocal description at the time (*'The deceased was a prostitute residing at Nuneaton.'*).[89] It is likely that Polly Button had been driven to prostitution by the harsh consequences of poverty. Given the need or desire to protect the reputation of her mother and the family, it comes as no surprise that, under cross-examination in court, Elizabeth denied suggestions that, *'her mother had been seen with, or gone out with, other persons or walked about the streets of Nuneaton with men other than John Danks.'* She said that no one but

> 'A single woman of loose character'

---

88   *Evening Mail* (London), 2 April 1832, p. 3; *Staffordshire Advertiser*, 7 April 1832, p. 2.
89   *Leicester Chronicle*, 7 April 1832.

Danks ever came to visit her mother and that she had never known her mother stay out all night before.

The issue and potential stigma of prostitution was shown when Elizabeth seems to have rebutted possible insinuations regarding herself: '*I am a ribbon weaver; I never walk about the streets of Nuneaton with men; I don't now; I had used to do so formerly.*' There would also appear to have been animosity between Elizabeth and John Danks: '*I never told other people I wished any harm would come to him; I only said I did not wish him to come to my mother, to bring more trouble on her; I told our landlady so; I never called him a scoundrel; never said I wished he was dead.*' On being questioned about her mother's state of mind, perhaps if she had been troubled in any way, Elizabeth had replied that her mother had '*not appeared melancholy of late*'. Indeed, given the recent filiation order and order for maintenance made by the Justices of the Peace against Danks at the start of the year, Polly could well have sensed some relief at the prospect of some desperately needed money to provide for her children.

Other witnesses also appear to have had their moral character questioned, James Green in particular. When questioned, he confirmed that he had been no stranger to the penal system. He stated that he had, '*been in a gaol more than once and more than twice. I believe I have been in three times.*' In fact, he had been indicted on a total of four occasions and had been found guilty on one of them, for stealing two geese and seven fowl,[90] which resulted in a prison sentence of twelve months. On the other three charges, including one of highway robbery and one of stealing two silver watches, he had eventually been acquitted, although not before spending several weeks in prison.[91] These criminal acts were no doubt driven by the destitution, hunger and despair that prevailed in Nuneaton in the few years around 1830.

---

90   *Leamington Spa Courier*, 12 December 1829, p. 3.
91   *Leamington Spa Courier*, 6 August 1831 & *Leamington Spa Courier*, 17 Dec 1831.

POST-MORTEM EXAMINATION OF THE BODY

Richard Lloyd was a surgeon who had been based in the town for just over three years, having arrived in August 1828. He had soon ruffled the feathers of two existing surgeons, Bucknill and Nason, by questioning their treatment methods and offering to undercut their charges. Bucknill and Nason won a successful libel action against him regarding the former in March 1830.[92] He had been a surgeon in the army, serving in England, Scotland, France and southern Europe. By way of passing literary interest, it is believed that the character of Tertius Lydgate in George Eliot's *Middlemarch* is influenced by Lloyd. On the morning of Sunday 19 February, Lloyd had been called in to examine Polly Button's body after it had been brought back to her house, perhaps because of his specific knowledge of lacerating wounds derived from his army service. He confirmed to the court that he had examined Polly Button's dead body that morning and that it had been kept in the same position on the door that she had been carried home on from the scene of the murder.

Lloyd's description of the wounds can be found in newspaper accounts of the trial and in a subsequent medical publication of 1843.[93] He was able to confirm that there was a noticeable bruise on Polly Button's left temple, presumably from where Danks had struck her with his right fist and knocked her to the floor. There were also three lacerations on Polly Button's body. The first wound described by Lloyd was that of a cut on the back of Polly Button's left hand, indicating most probably that she had initially used it to try to fend off Danks's first slash. The remaining two cuts were to Polly Button's throat. The less substantial one was a relatively superficial wound about one inch above the collar bone, where only the skin tissue had been cut through and the cartilage of the trachea had been grazed slightly. Lloyd thought that from such a wound, the quantity of blood in the hovel could never, by any possibility, have flowed. His opinion, therefore, was that the second cut to Polly Button's throat, inflicted two inches above the first cut, had been the wound that resulted in her death. As regards this wound, Lloyd

92   *Warwick and Warwickshire Advertiser*, 3 April 1830, p. 3.
93   Taylor, p. 441.

had observed at the upper part of the throat, near the left angle of the jaw, a gaping cut about seven inches in length and three inches in depth. It extended backwards to the commencement of the oesophagus and passed obliquely down the right side of the neck as far as the fourth cervical vertebra. The trunk of the carotid artery and all the principal branches of the external carotid, with the jugulars, had been severed. Lloyd gave evidence that in his opinion such a wound must have occasioned death within a very short time and that the knife previously presented as belonging to Danks could have inflicted the wounds he had described. Lloyd had thought it highly improbable, although not impossible, that Polly Button could have travelled the distance of twenty-three yards, besides getting over the gate, in such a condition.

The severing of the carotid artery and other blood vessels in Polly Button's neck, when coupled with the stress and terror she must have experienced in the attack by Danks and the considerable exertion in making her way out of the barn, would inevitably have resulted in both rapid blood loss and a drop in blood pressure. Despite apparent efforts by Polly Button to use her cap to staunch the flow of blood, the consequent loss of oxygen to the critical organs of the brain and the heart would have led to Polly Button losing consciousness within a minute or so of exiting the barn, followed by cardiac arrest and her death.[94]

Given the description of the mortal wound, Danks must have exerted considerable force as he pulled the knife downwards across her neck from his position on top of her back. Little wonder perhaps that descriptions such as *'cut the head almost off'* and *'head nearly severed from the body'* were given in newspaper reports. An illustration by a leading US medical illustrator that shows the two cuts to Polly Button's throat was commissioned for this book and is shown in Figure 28.

Lloyd then went on to confirm that Polly Button had been pregnant (*'in the family way, and far advanced'*) and that he had been present when the footmarks had been compared by Constable

---

94   Email correspondence (18 February 2019, the anniversary of Polly Button's murder) from Dr Stephen Heap (incidentally, a direct descendant of John Danks).

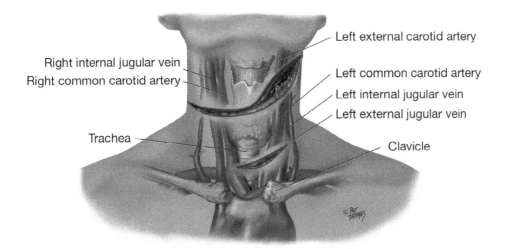

Right internal jugular vein
Right common carotid artery

Left external carotid artery

Left common carotid artery

Left internal jugular vein

Left external jugular vein

Trachea

Clavicle

Haddon. He was cross-examined as to the likelihood that someone with such injuries would have been able to get over the locked four-barred gate – which was some 3 feet 10 inches in height[95] – leading to and from the hovel. Newspaper reports show some variation in recording his response – with one being, '*I should think it improbable she could have got over a gate*', while another records, '*It was not highly improbable for a person to be able to get over a gate, and to get to some distance.*' A variation in newspaper reports can also be noted in his response to the next question under cross-examination: '*he had known of a person committing suicide and, with the carotid artery and jugular vein cut, being able to walk a distance of 70 yards*' compared with '*I have known a person who committed suicide to have run 15 yards*'. The press reports of Lloyd's evidence concluded with his statement that Polly Button, '*after the wound had been inflicted, would not have been able to cry out so as to be heard at a distance of a quarter of an inch.*' With a savage slash of his knife, Danks had certainly '*stopped her hooting*'.

It is at this point in the telling of the story of Polly Button's murder, that it is worth noting that the case subsequently achieved much wider, indeed international, recognition. This interest began with lectures and articles by Andrew Amos, prosecuting counsel. Aspects of the Polly Button murder case were included in his

Fig. 28.
Illustration showing the two cuts to Polly Button's throat.
©Pat Thomas 2018.

95   Taylor, p. 442.

increasingly popular law lectures at London University and in an article featured in the *London Medical Gazette* in May 1832.[96] Awareness of the case widened further due to its inclusion in major textbooks on medico-legal issues, both by Alfred Swaine Taylor in the UK[97] and by Theodric Romeyn Beck and his brother John Brodhead Beck in the USA,[98] in works both entitled *Elements of Medical Jurisprudence*. Taylor was an English toxicologist and medical writer who has been described as the 'father of British forensic medicine'. By coincidence, it would appear that Taylor and Justice James Parke, the trial judge, became good friends in later years after Parke received a pamphlet from Taylor on the case of an alleged poisoning. In reply Parke acknowledged '*the necessity for the most scrupulous care in considering medical testimony*' (as had been the case in Danks's trial) and how much the legal system was indebted to Taylor for his influential contribution to medical jurisprudence[99] – being the study and application of scientific and medical knowledge in a legal context.

The key issue of medical jurisprudence arising from the murder that was raised in such respected publications was how rapidly death may have occurred and whether Polly Button would have been capable of moving from the scene of the attack under her own volition. This arose from the consideration at the trial of evidence as to whether Polly Button would have been capable of walking the twenty-three yards from the hovel, in the process also climbing over the four-barred gate, to where she eventually dropped from exhaustion and died in the roadway, given the severity of her injuries. The following is a summary of the pertinent trial evidence that will help address this question.

The circumstances of the murder merit particular scrutiny. Was it certain that Danks really did inflict the fatal wound in the hovel, or could it have been on the spot where the body was found? And if the former, it seemed extraordinary that after such a wound, in which the main trunk of the carotid, its external branches, and the jugulars, were severed, that Polly Button was still able to get

---

96 Amos, pp. 183–86.
97 Taylor, pp. 439–43.
98 Beck & Beck, p. 346.
99 Letter from James Parke to Alfred S Taylor, 22 January 1849.

up and travel such a distance. The opinion of Richard Lloyd, the examining surgeon, that such a movement and travel distance was improbable though not impossible, would most likely have reflected the opinions of expert witnesses of the time. However, the conclusion of subsequent analyses reported by Amos, Taylor and the Beck brothers was that when all the trial's forensic evidence, facts and circumstances of the case were put together, no other conclusion can be drawn other than Danks's declaration must have been true. This would have meant that the wounds were inflicted in the hovel and that, despite such a severe and bloody assault, Polly Button had been able to get to her feet, stagger through the hovel, clamber over the gate and stumble onwards to the place in the adjacent roadway where she fell at last from utter exhaustion.

Amos's article in the *London Medical Gazette* went into some further detail regarding the evidence about the wounds: '*The first wound, as Mr. Buchanan had evidenced, was quite inconsiderable. On the other hand, it would seem that there had been from the second wound a most copious flow of blood, which was thrown off by the prominence of her belly (she being far advanced in pregnancy) to the side of the hovel, as she passed along to the gate; then on the gate a similar transfer of blood was manifest, and there also were the marks of both her hands. The prisoner's hand was also marked on the gate, but at a different place.*'[100]

James Williams Buchanan was a lawyer, one of Nuneaton's most prominent citizens and, along with others, had supported Constable Haddon in gathering information and evidence about the circumstances of the murder after Danks had been arrested. Another George Eliot literary connection can be established here. It is thought that Eliot based the character of the bullying and heavy-drinking lawyer Robert Dempster in *Janet's Repentance*, the final story within Eliot's *Scenes of Clerical Life*, on him. Buchanan had first looked at the site soon after the murder and was puzzled by his observation that there had scarcely been any blood between the gate and where Polly Button had collapsed in the roadway. He had accounted for this by her using the cap she had been wearing to staunch the flow of blood from the wounds to her neck and

---

100 Amos, p. 185.

compressing them still further by holding down her head as she struggled in vain to get back home to her children. There was, however, a large quantity of blood found to have flowed down between her breasts and congealed about her pubic region. It had accumulated to such an extent, indeed, that the women who removed the clothing from the body thought at first that there must have been an attempt made to remove the foetus, although this was shown not to be the case upon medical examination. The examining surgeon, Richard Lloyd, had also noted that there had been a great absorption of blood by the undergarments worn by Polly Button.

Buchanan had revisited the crime scene on the Sunday after the trial, 1 April 1832, to try to establish timings for what had taken place. It had taken him fifteen seconds to pass from the spot where the wound was inflicted in the hovel, climb over the gate, and to walk to the place where the body was found. In a subsequent experiment, taken at a slower pace, it took him twenty seconds. The obstruction of the gate, he thought, might have added another nine seconds or so given the state Polly Button was in. To more accurately estimate how much time had elapsed from the time the wound was inflicted on Polly Button until she collapsed in the roadway, subsequent reviewers felt that other considerations also needed to be taken into account. Consequently, the twenty-nine seconds or so calculated by Buchanan were thought to be short of the actual time. Starting from the moment in which Danks had '*stopped her hooting*', having probably divided the trachea and severing the great blood vessels of Polly's neck, Danks would have arisen from his prostrate position and, having left her for dead, made his way hurriedly home. Polly Button, in the meantime, must be supposed to have lain tranquil, at least while Danks was in the hovel. Somehow, and incredibly, Polly Button then seems to have rallied herself, got to her feet and set herself in motion in the direction along which she was traced the following day by Constable Haddon and others. Such an elemental display of the force of self-preservation and maternal instinct, to get back to look after her young children, is remarkable, if not to say heroic. It could not have been done in an instant; on the contrary, several seconds, perhaps at least ten more, must have passed. This allowance would therefore give an approximate total approaching 40 seconds from the end of Danks's attack to when Polly Button collapsed in the roadway. Consequently, it is not merely the time of crossing the gate that should be considered but also the delay until Danks had left the hovel, the impact of the expenditure of effort and energy, and the loss of blood that must have occurred in accomplishing this incredible feat.

Summing up by the Judge, Verdict and Sentence

All witnesses having been heard, all that was left for Justice Parke to do was to sum up the evidence to the jury. He observed that it now became *'their painful duty to consider, deeply and impartially, the case between the prisoner and the country.'* Parke reiterated that Danks was charged with the highest crime – *'that of shedding the blood of a fellow creature'* – and it consequently required their most deliberate consideration before they consigned the prisoner to an ignominious death. It was their duty to consider all the circumstances of the case and if, in the course of their investigation of those circumstances, there arose any reasonable doubt in their minds, they would need to acquit the prisoner.

He stated that there was no doubt that at half-past seven on the evening of *'this dreadful occurrence'*, Polly Button had been alone in the company of Danks and that circumstantial evidence had been produced which had fully described the manner in which she had met her death. Parke confirmed that, given the evidence, he thought there could arise no possible doubt that the deceased had come to her death by violent means. He concluded by focusing the jury's mind on the key question: who had been the person who had inflicted the blows that had caused her death? The confession of Danks standing before them in the dock was confirmed by all the circumstances of the evidence that had been produced by Constable Haddon and if they were satisfied with his testimony and believed that he had spoken the truth, they must find Danks guilty.

The jury then retired to consider the evidence they had heard. The wait for a decision was not a long one, as almost immediately the twelve-man jury came back into court and George Powell, the foreman, announced a verdict of guilty. The brevity of the jury's deliberations surely confirms the overwhelming nature of the evidence against Danks that had been presented in court

The clerk of arraigns had then called upon the prisoner to say why sentence of death should not be passed upon him, to which he answered, *'I'm not guilty'.*

As tradition dictated when passing the death sentence, Justice Parke then proceeded to remove the black cap from the hook attached to his canopied chair, placed the cap on his head and gave this solemn address to Danks, who stood silently in the dock:

> *That awful moment has now arrived when you are about to receive from the offended justice of your country that sentence which it assigns to enormous guilt like yours. You have been convicted on the clearest evidence and upon your own confession of your guilt, confirmed by a variety of circumstances in the case…all of which must bring everyone to the conclusion that you are the wicked man who has destroyed the life of a fellow creature. Your guilt appears as clear from the evidence in this case as if we had seen it with our own eyes, that you induced her to the place where you have been before, carrying on your wicked intercourse with her, and that she went when she suspected nothing of this kind from you. You there betrayed her cruelly and ungratefully, and committed that crime which you had before designed in your heart, and inflicted upon her instant death. In the whole course of my experience, I have never heard a case in which so much brutality and cruelty has been evinced. It is highly impossible for me to hold out to you the slightest hope of any mercy to be extended to you on this side of the grave.*
>
> *It has pleased God to open your heart to some little repentance, by relieving your mind to the reverend clergymen who attended to you; let me entreat you still to endeavour by sincere repentance to procure, at the hands of the Almighty, that pardon which it is utterly impossible for the interest of those that live to extend to you in this world. I exhort you to employ that small remaining portion of your existence (for it will be very short) in prayer and repentance to obtain remission of your sins.*
>
> *I entreat you to avail yourself of that assistance which will be afforded you by the reverend gentlemen who attend the gaol. Employ*

your time well and be assured it is impossible for you to be permitted
to live.

It now only remains for me to pass that sentence which it is my
bounden duty to do, which is that you be removed from hence to the
place you came, and thence on Monday next to the place of execution,
that you there be hanged by the neck until you are dead, and that your
body be taken down and be delivered to the surgeons for dissection,
according to the statutes made and provided, And may the Lord have
mercy on your soul.

Of particular importance in Justice Parke's address is the statement
that Danks had '*committed that crime which you had before designed*
in your heart'. This confirms that Danks had invited Polly Button
out for the walk on that fateful evening with malice aforethought,
i.e. he was either definitely intent on her murder or was willing
to resort to murder if he could not find a way to resolve their
difficulties over maintenance payments.

Danks listened to Parke's address without any emotion and
as he was leaving the dock said, in a firm and loud voice to Mr
Haddon, who was present in the courtroom, '*Thank you, Mr*
Haddon'.

The Execution of John Danks

THE PROCESS OF JUDICIAL HANGING

Danks would have been executed by 'short-drop' hanging, the
method most widely used at the time. Such hangings were
also usually carried out in public. In short-drop hanging the
condemned prisoner would have been suspended by the removal of
the platform on which they stood by the release of a trapdoor drop
mechanism, a system that had been used in Britain from 1760.
Short-drop hanging drops the prisoner just a few inches (typically
twelve). There is insufficient force to beak the spine and the noose
rapidly constricts the neck just below the jawline by as much as a
third. Compression of the carotid arteries and jugular veins starves
the brain of oxygen and stops the flow of blood within the head,
respectively. Crushing the carotid sinuses, a group of nerves in

close proximity to the carotid arteries, may result in such powerful stimulation of the vagus nerve that the heart slows to a stop. Constriction of the hyoid bone and larynx crushes and occludes the airway, causing suffocation. What follows would be a loss of consciousness, which can be lost in as little as eight to ten seconds or as much as a minute, and a stage of convulsions where the face becomes distorted and livid, the eyes become prominent, and there is violent struggling, typically for one to three minutes. Death is usually caused by a combination of asphyxia (the constricting force of the rope causes compressive narrowing of the larynx and trachea, forcing up the roof of the tongue against the back of the pharynx and folding the epiglottis over the entrance of the larynx to block the airway) and cerebral hypoxia (compressive blockage of the jugular veins that stops the circulation of blood through the brain and starves it of oxygen).[101] After breathing ceases, brain death occurs in around six minutes and the heart stops beating within 10–15 minutes.

The 'long-drop' method, or measured drop, was not used in England until 1872 where it was used at Lincoln prison. It is considered to be a more humane method of hanging, as it is designed to break the prisoner's neck by allowing them to fall a pre-determined distance.[102] This Official Table of Drops was used until the last hanging in the United Kingdom in 1965.

SAMUEL HAYWOOD – THE HANGMAN

Samuel Haywood was an agricultural labourer from Appleby Magna, Leicestershire, who had been arrested and charged in March 1817 with being equipped for poaching and having snares and other instruments for the destruction of game. On Friday, 18 April 1817, Haywood was tried, convicted and sentenced to two years imprisonment in the county Bridewell House of Correction in High Cross Street, Leicester.[103] It was during his spell in prison that he volunteered to flog another prisoner.

---

101 Email correspondence from Dr Stephen Heap, 18 February 2019.
102 Clarke.
103 *The Leicester Chronicle*, 19 April 1817.

The prison governor offered Haywood the vacant position of hangman for Leicestershire, Derbyshire and Nottinghamshire. His earliest recorded execution was that of Thomas Wilcox at Nottingham on 24 March 1820 and in his subsequent career he executed at least 44 people, including three women. Haywood travelled as far afield as Gloucester and Liverpool, such was his reputation for hanging. He carried out triple hangings in Nottingham in 1822 and Derby in 1843, and a double hanging in Lancaster in 1832. In fact, the spring of 1832 proved to be a busy period for Haywood, as after hanging Sarah Smith in Leicester on 26 March, just a few days later, on Monday 2 April, he was in action in Warwick where he was the hangman at the execution of John Danks. Haywood's final execution was that of John Platts at Derby gaol on 1 April 1847. The rope used at Platts' hanging has been preserved for posterity in Scotland Yard's Metropolitan Police Museum in London.

NEWSPAPER COVERAGE

Newspapers concluded their coverage of the story of Polly Button's murder with accounts of Danks's last few days in prison and his execution by hanging three days after the trial on Monday 2 April outside the lodge and in front of Warwick County Gaol – see Figures 29 and 30. On his return to prison, after being condemned to death by Justice Parke, '*he had behaved with the most sincere contrition, acknowledging the justice of his punishment and listening with becoming attention to the pious exhortations of the Chaplain* [the Rev. George Childe] *who administered to him, with his customary humanity, all the consolation of which his situation required.*' While in prison his conduct remained peaceable and exemplary. On Saturday 31 March, he had met with his wife for the last time and bid her a painful goodbye. Danks seems to have maintained his composure, '*which he had done both immediately before and after his trial, not having allowed himself to indulge in the hope of a mitigation of that punishment, which awaited his human depravity and accumulated guilt.*'[104]

---

104 *Leamington Spa Courier*, 7 April 1832, p. 3.

Over his final weekend, Danks was reported to have exhibited a dread of his approaching doom. He had made references to the sound of the footsteps he had heard as he had fled from the murder scene, perhaps in his somewhat disturbed state thinking that they had been those of Polly Button after she had somehow risen from the floor of the hovel and climbed over the four-barred gate to the roadway. In fact, it seems quite possible that the noises that Danks heard that night could well have been those made by Polly Button as she staggered and clambered over the gate by the hovel in her vain attempt to reach home. Danks remained unable to see how she had managed this feat, given that he had left her for dead.

The press reported that Danks expressed himself as greatly indebted to Constable Haddon for his kindness to him while in custody previous to his committal to gaol and also for his attention to his wife while he had been confined. He also said he was quite satisfied with the manner in which Mr Haddon had given his testimony at the trial, saying that he had spoken nothing but the truth – somewhat at odds with what Danks had stated in court.

Fig. 29. The site of Danks's execution – outside Warwick gaol, Barrack Street, Warwick.

At seven o'clock on the morning of the execution, the concourse in front of the gaol was already very crowded, the presence of the monthly Warwick cattle fair greatly contributing to the number of onlookers. Many in the crowd had travelled from Nuneaton to witness the execution of their unfortunate townsman. While the crowd gathered outside the gaol at this hour, Danks was attending the prison chapel, where the usual condemnation service was being read by the chaplain. The condemnation service finished at eight o'clock. The female prisoners were the first to leave the chapel, passing through the courtyard from which they could clearly see the newly-erected scaffold through the archway. The debtors followed next, followed a few minutes later by the chaplain and a very grave-looking Danks, who gave a melancholy look towards the scaffold upon which he was shortly to be hanged. He was then taken to the press-room, where he gave his thanks to Mr Adkins, the Governor of Warwick gaol, and the chaplain for their kindness towards him, and where his arms were pinioned in preparation for the hanging.

Fig. 30.
Illustration of the scaffold in front of Warwick Gaol in Marden's *The Murder of Polly Button*.

With everything now in readiness, the solemn tolling of the bells of the nearby St Mary's Church marked the signal for the procession to the scaffold to begin. Danks was led by the Under Sheriff and the prison governor across the courtyard and into a lobby next to the prison lodge. It was from here, at about twenty minutes past eight, that Danks walked the short distance to the scaffold and mounted it unaided. He was reported to have groaned deeply when he had caught sight of the rope that was very shortly to end his life. He appeared to have been recently crying, and onlookers reported that he looked to be suffering from bursts of mental anguish and fearful apprehension of what lay ahead. Danks was placed under the beam where the rope had been fixed and for the few remaining seconds of his life he prayed repeatedly, '*Oh, God, receive my soul, the Lord receive my soul*'. When the cap was drawn over his eyes, he was heard to repeat his prayer more loudly, his last words before the fatal platform fell from beneath his feet being '*Lord receive my soul*'. He struggled a great deal – his legs flailing, his hands clenching, and bearing down his arms extremely hard for a few seconds. Some two minutes elapsed before Danks ceased to move and about five minutes before he was pronounced dead. His body, after hanging for an appropriate length of time, was cut down and delivered over to two men from

Fig. 31. Entry in the Nuneaton Diary for 13 April 1832 recording the execution of Danks.

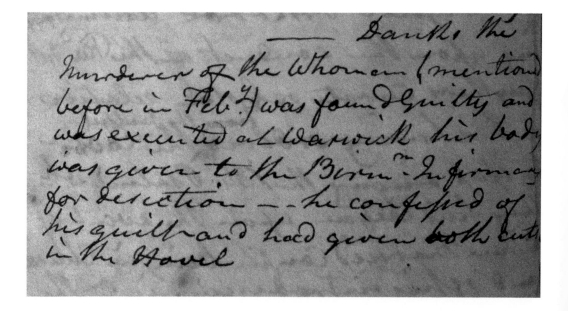

the Birmingham Medical School, who were to transport his body there for dissection.

The news of Danks being found guilty, his hanging and the transportation of his body for dissection to the Birmingham Medical School was duly recorded by John Astley of Nuneaton in his diary entry for 13 April 1832, see Figure 31. The diary entry reads: '*Danks the murderer of the whoman (mentioned before in Feby.) was found Guilty and was executed at Warwick his body was given to the Birmm. Infirmary for dissection… he confessed of his guilt and had given both cuts in the Hovel.*'

Fig. 32.
Trials Broadside 331: Life, Trial and Execution of John Danks (Historical and Special Collections, Harvard Law School Library).

RARE HISTORICAL DOCUMENT ASSOCIATED WITH THE EXECUTION OF DANKS

In addition to newspaper coverage, there was a market for speedily produced 'execution broadsides' – a sheet of paper printed on one side only, comprising one large page without columns. Just as programmes are sold at concerts and sporting events today, broadsides – styled at the time as '*Last Dying Speeches*' or '*Bloody Murders*' – were sold to the audiences that gathered to witness public executions in eighteenth- and nineteenth-century Britain. These ephemeral publications were intended for the middle or lower classes and most sold for a penny or less. Published in British towns and cities by printers who specialised in this type of street literature, a typical example would feature an illustration (usually of the criminal, the crime scene or the execution), an account of the crime and, sometimes, the trial and the purported confession of the criminal often cautioning the reader to avoid the fate awaiting the perpetrator.

The Harvard Law School Library in Cambridge, Massachusetts, has a collection

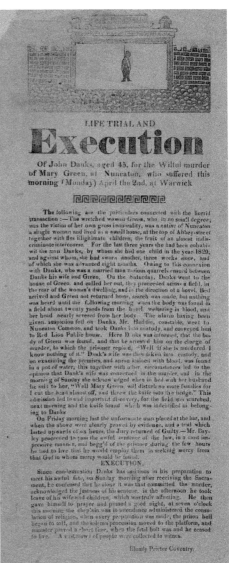

of more than 500 broadsides, giving accounts of executions for such crimes as arson, assault, counterfeiting, horse stealing, murder, rape, robbery, and treason. Within its archive is a copy of a broadside pertaining to the execution of John Danks for the murder of Polly Button (Figure 32). A local printer from Coventry, Blomly, had been quick to produce a broadside, entitled *Life, Trial and Execution of John Danks*, that incorporated a rather grisly engraving of a prisoner hanged at a scaffold. A transcript of Danks's execution broadside is given in Annexe 4.

The Dissection of John Danks

BACKGROUND

In England, dissection remained entirely prohibited until the 16th century, when a series of Royal Edicts gave specific groups of physicians and surgeons some limited rights to dissect cadavers. The permission was quite restricted. For example, in 1540, Henry VIII had given the Company of Barber-Surgeons the right to the bodies of four hanged criminals per year. By the mid-eighteenth century, the Company of Barber-Surgeons and the Royal College of Physicians were the only two groups permitted to carry out dissections and had an annual quota of ten cadavers between them. As a result of pressure from anatomists, especially in the rapidly growing medical schools, the Murder Act 1752 allowed judges the discretion to permit the bodies of executed murderers to be dissected for anatomical research and education. The Act included the provision: '*for better preventing the horrid crime of murder, that some further terror and peculiar mark of infamy be added to the punishment.*' The Act also stipulated that a person found guilty of murder should be executed two days after being sentenced unless that day was a Sunday, in which case the execution would take place on the following Monday, as was the case with John Danks.

Although this period coincided with an increase in the number of crimes attracting the death sentence, the actual number of executions that took place fell, so that by the nineteenth century the supply of cadavers proved insufficient due to both the continuing expansion of medical schools and consequent increase in students of anatomy. A thriving black market arose in cadavers and body parts, leading, in the extreme, to the infamous Burke and Hare murders over a period of ten months in Edinburgh in 1828, when 16 people were murdered in order to sell their cadavers to anatomists. The resulting public outcry largely led to the passage of the Anatomy Act 1832, which greatly increased the legal supply of cadavers for dissection. The Act was passed by the House of Lords on 19 July 1832. Danks was therefore one of the last criminals convicted of murder to be sentenced to hanging followed by dissection. There were only two others after Danks: John/Jonathan Smithers (9 July) and Thomas Reilly (11 July), both hanged at Newgate prison in London.

THE DISSECTING SURGEON – WILLIAM SANDS COX – AND THE BIRMINGHAM SCHOOL OF MEDICINE

William Sands Cox (1802–1875) (Figure 33) was a surgeon who had worked to establish a school of medicine in Birmingham. In 1825, he was appointed surgeon to the General Dispensary in Birmingham and gave his first lecture on anatomy, with physiological and surgical observations, at 12 noon on 1 December of that year at his father's house, 24 Temple Row. He became surgeon to the town's infirmary in 1827. In October 1828, after a good deal of opposition and in conjunction with fellow doctors, he founded the Birmingham School of Medicine and Surgery. Cox subsequently lectured on both anatomy and surgery.

The rapidly increasing number of medical students led to a move to larger premises in Snow Hill, Birmingham. Opening on 18 October 1829, the premises were located in Brittle Street, near its junction with Livery Street. It was to these premises that Danks's body was transported after his hanging, where it was subsequently dissected as part of a series

Fig. 33. William Sands Cox, 1854.

of four lectures delivered by Cox on the inner workings of the human body.

THE DISSECTION LECTURES

At least one newspaper[105] covered the dissection of Danks, reporting that the body had been exhibited to a considerable number of persons at the Medical School on Tuesday 3 April and Wednesday 4 April. On the latter evening, Cox had given the first of his four lectures, with accompanying dissection, to a lecture room filled to overflowing. In addition to the medical students, it was said that '*a very large number of the inhabitants went to see the sight, even quite young boys being admitted*'.[106] The subject of the first lecture had been the structure of the alimentary canal/digestive tract and the physiology of digestion. This had been quickly followed by a lecture on the structure of the heart and the physiology of the circulation of the blood. On the following Monday evening (9 April), Danks's body was the subject of a lecture on the structure of the lungs and the physiology of respiration. The short lecture series concluded on Wednesday 11 April with a dissection giving a general view of the nervous system.

The public dissection of John Danks concludes this chapter in the telling of Polly Button's story. The relationship that Polly Button had sustained with John Danks had lasted longer than with any other partner. It would appear that there had existed some caring or affectionate bond between the two of them, but this had proved insufficient against the bitter winds of depression and destitution sweeping through Nuneaton as its silk ribbon weaving industry collapsed. As their situation had become ever more desperate, on that cold February evening in 1832 Danks had lured Polly Button on a walk to Astley's hovel, a place of familiar intimacy for them. Danks's bloody and pre-meditated attack on Polly Button had led to his own sad end on a dissecting table in Birmingham, the inevitable consequence of the intentionally shameful 'double punishment' sentence that had been imposed by Justice Parke.

---

105 *The Coventry Herald*, 13 April 1832.
106 Wilkinson, p. 28.

THE TIES THAT BIND

Ripples from the Past – Places and People

Introduction

What is it about the murder of Polly Button that has maintained
the interest of Nuneatonians through the generations since 1832?
In the absence of many physical reminders, we are fortunate to have
seen the story passed on in a variety of ways. Foremost amongst
these is via the oral tradition – that is, through conversations
between people as members of families, of communities, and of
local history and family history groups. The story has also been
perpetuated by the publication of occasional newspaper articles,
Marden's landmark first printed account of the murder in 1977
(*The Murder of Polly Button*), and three plays performed locally
almost 150 years apart. The murder also resulted in a memorable
skipping rhyme, thereby ensuring younger generations continued
to hear about the story:

> Johnny Danks, he played his pranks
> Upon poor Polly Button.
> He drew his knife, to please his wife,
> And cut her up like mutton.

The tragic life and brutal murder of Polly Button has consequently
remained in the consciousness of people in Nuneaton for almost

two centuries. Of course, the echoes and ripples of the past can fade with time, but it is hoped that the collective memory of Polly's desperately sad story can now also be sustained by recognising the physical ties that exist within the town's streets and through a family tree of descendants that reaches to us over the generations. Research was therefore undertaken to identify the locations of key buildings and places of significance in the story. In addition, a natural and consequential interest in finding out what happened to Polly Button's children led to the tracing of as many of Polly Button's descendants as could be established from her five children through to the present-day. In pursuing what is probably a unique line of research in a project such as this, it is hoped that the story of Polly Button can also be brought to the attention of hundreds, if not thousands, of her direct descendants.

Ripples: Places

Naturally, the brutal slaying of a woman who was very advanced in pregnancy would have created considerable shock throughout the town. The ripples of such a dreadful event would perhaps be capable of being sustained more easily and effectively through the physical fabric of actual buildings that might survive from that age. However, other than St Nicolas Parish Church, none of the buildings of relevance in the story have survived. It would have been in and around these buildings that the townsfolk would have gathered to express their shock and disbelief, to gawk and gossip about the murder, and to attend or eavesdrop on the inquest that was held into Polly Button's death. Research to identify the location of key buildings has been carried out in the hope that this will allow the better appreciation, if not visualisation, of the events that took place. I have found this to be the case personally. I drive past the location of Polly Button's house most days as I travel to and from work; probably on a weekly basis I pass over the place where she died; when I walk through certain parts of Nuneaton's town centre I can identify where Danks had been taken to after his arrest, where he had been held in the town's gaol, and where he had appeared in front of the inquest jury. By identifying the precise location of key buildings and events it is hoped that readers will also be able to enhance their understanding of the historical fabric of Nuneaton.

Polly Button's house was located in what is now (2019) a car park at the rear of a small run of shops at the junction of Upper Abbey Street and Friary Street. Previously, the site had been that of the Wheatsheaf public house. Using new georeferenced maps (Figs. 27 & 38) **John Danks's house** has been calculated to have been just 76 metres away from Polly Button's house. The approximate locations of both houses are shown in Figure 34.

In the 1888 Ordnance Survey map of Nuneaton, **Astley's hovel**, the site of Danks's murderous attack, had already achieved notoriety with the barn now being known as Polly Button's Barn (Figure 35). After exiting the barn, Polly Button had eventually collapsed and died some 21 metres away in the adjacent pathway. In present-day terms, this would place the spot where she died as being in St Marys Road between the Sandon Road and Aston Road junctions.

The Red Lion public house, where Danks was first taken by Constable Haddon after his arrest, is shown in Figure 36. It was located at the point where Wash Lane narrowed as it approached Market Place, in the vicinity of what is now 6 Queens Road, Nuneaton. It should be noted that the Red Lion public house that features prominently in *Janet's Repentance* in George Eliot's *Scenes of Clerical Life* – set in the fictional town of Milby and based on Nuneaton – is not the Red Lion where Danks was first detained. Eliot's fictional Red Lion was actually based on The Bull Hotel (now The George Eliot) in Bridge Street, Nuneaton.

Above: **Fig. 34.** Junction of Friary Street and Abbey Street, Nuneaton, showing approximate locations of Polly Button's house and John Danks's house.

Below: **Fig. 35.** 1888 Ordnance Survey map of Nuneaton showing location of Astley's hovel, then called Polly Button's Barn, circled.

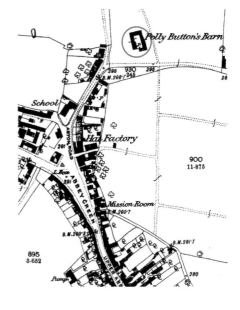

Above: **Fig. 36.** The Red Lion public house – original building and present-day view of where it would have been located.

Below: **Fig. 37.** The location where The Britannia public house stood in 1832, in Abbey Street, Nuneaton.

The Britannia public house, where the inquest was held three days after the murder, is also long gone. It was located at what is now present-day 117/117A Abbey Street, see Figure 37.

All key locations in Nuneaton mentioned at the trial were included in the map presented to the jury. By georeferencing the trial map, it has been possible to commission a new map for this publication that shows these locations as an overlay onto the present-day layout of the town – see Figure 38. That part of the route taken by Danks on the night of the murder is shown as it was indicated on the original map, although it is worth noting that the trial map did not show the full route as described by Danks to Constable Haddon, i.e. the reconnoitring of the barn first had been omitted. In addition, there could have been some slight inaccuracies in the original map in view of its hasty preparation for the trial. In present-day terms, the most likely route that can be suggested for Danks to have followed on his way to reconnoitre the barn on the night he murdered Polly Button would have been: Burgage Place, Corporation Street, Graham Street, Central Avenue, Sandon Road, and then St Mary's Road.

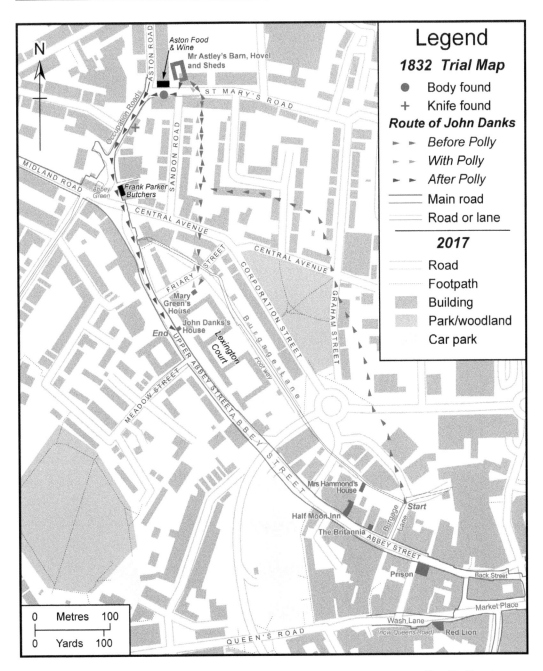

Fig. 38. Key elements of the map used at Danks's trial overlaid onto the present-day layout of Nuneaton.

Birmingham Medical School, where Danks had been dissected, was the last building of significance to be located, and proved slightly more of a challenge. Located in Brittle Street, Birmingham, the building had only been used as a medical school between 1829 and 1834. With the coming of the Railway Age – and specifically Birmingham Station, which opened in 1852 and was renamed Snow Hill Station in 1858, and the Birmingham, Wolverhampton and Dudley Railway line, which opened in 1854 – the Medical School and the rest of Brittle Street had been lost to development. However, from an analysis of maps at Birmingham Archives[107] and the National Archives[108], it can now be confirmed that the location of the Medical School was in the region of the present-day car park at Snow Hill Station, off Livery Street (Figure 39).

Fig. 39.
Location where the Birmingham Medical School building was sited between 1829 and 1834.

107 Map of Birmingham from the survey made in 1824 and 1825, by J. Pigott Smith (1824-1825) (Birmingham: Archives, Heritage and Photography Service – MS 3700/2/1).

108 Plan showing area around Brittle Street, Snow Hill in Birmingham; shows position of properties belonging to Houghton, Hales and Aston, petitioners against the Great Western Railway (Stratford Line, etc.) (The National Archives – RAIL 1196/11).

Ripples: People (The Descendants of Polly Button)

 The Phone Book

 **rightmove** ⌂

Having identified key locations of relevance to the story of Polly Button, such physical aspects can now be supplemented by consideration of the social and familial consequences for her five children: Elizabeth, William, Hannah, Ann and Jane. The development of the internet since Cyril Marden wrote his book in the 1970s has revolutionised genealogical research to an extent that he could probably never have imagined. Using several websites and Record Offices, it has been possible to research what happened to Polly Button's children after she had been murdered and then to trace their descendants through to the present-day. The research initially focussed on tracing descendants using online subscription memberships of two of the largest genealogy sites (Ancestry and Find My Past), supplemented occasionally with the free-to-use FamilySearch site provided by The Church of Jesus Christ of Latter-day Saints. Experienced genealogists will be aware of the need to cross-reference and verify all people and events. Although the explosion in the popularity of researching one's family history in recent years has resulted in many family trees being built up and made accessible on the online genealogy sites, many of those containing parts of the Polly Button family tree were found to be incomplete or have errors within them. Perhaps unusually for a family tree, which typically starts off with a living person and is then traced backwards, researching and creating Polly Button's family tree in Ancestry started with Polly Button herself and then worked forwards in time to the present-day. Care was taken to ensure, as far as possible, that the available records of any individual potentially identified as being a descendant were corroborated/verified and 'made sense' when seen in conjunction with other records pertaining to that branch of the family tree.

The genealogical records that were found to be of most use as a source of key information were the national censuses from 1841 to 1911, the 1939 National Register, parish registers of baptisms, marriages and burials, and details of records of births, marriages and deaths post-1837 held by the General Register Office. The online genealogy sites also contained a wide range of other records that provided additional and sometimes critical information when tracing certain individuals, for example military records, electoral rolls, travel and migration records, phone directories, social directories, and school admission books. The 1939 Register proved to be an extremely useful resource, as it is the only national census-type resource currently available that bridges the gap between 1911 and 1951. The register was therefore instrumental in helping to trace recent generations and provided a vital link to help identify living descendants.

Identifying and confirming individuals' details in more recent times was further aided by using search engines such as Google, newspaper archives, online phone directories, electoral roll information from the subscription website People Trace UK, and social media sites such as Facebook.

The following table summarises the outcome of the genealogical research that was undertaken.

Child	Number of direct descendants traced	Of which number were identified as living descendants
Elizabeth	984	476
William	0	0
Hannah	667	363
Ann	202	81
Jane	275	134
TOTAL	**2,128**	**1,054**

Establishing an accurate and comprehensive family tree for the descendants of a murdered person is probably a unique piece of research. The detective work involved in tracing the descendants of Polly Button required diligence and tenacity in order to assess, validate and collate a wide variety of information together into a coherent and fully evidenced family tree. Using the information that had been gathered and verified, it subsequently became possible to contact identified direct descendants using a variety of means – including Facebook Messenger, letter, email and telephone – to inform them of their connection to Polly Button. The response to hearing of the connection to Polly Button was overwhelmingly positive, with the vast majority keen to know more about her story. This is where social media has shown how beneficial it can be in linking people who share a common interest – or in this case a common ancestor. A closed (private) Facebook group, The Descendants of Polly Button (https://www. facebook.com/groups/DescendantsOfPollyButton) was created in February 2017, followed by the creation of a public Facebook group, The Undoing of Polly Button, in December 2017 (https:// www.facebook.com/groups/UndoingOfPollyButton). The growth in the membership of both groups is testament to the continued interest in the murder of Polly Button specifically and the desire to know more about the history of Nuneaton in more general terms. Indeed, descendants were keen to visit Nuneaton to find out more about the story behind Polly Button's murder. As a consequence, the first ever 'gatherings' of descendants of Polly Button took place on 17 and 18 February 2019, in commemoration of the anniversary of her murder. Dozens of descendants travelled from across the country to hear the first full public presentations of the background to Polly Button's life and her murder at the hands of John Danks, followed by guided walks showing key locations and the route taken by Danks on the night in question.

The extensive research to trace the descendants of Polly Button through her five children was concentrated over a relatively short period. As a result, the general similarity and rhythm of people's lives over the generations became very apparent. From birth to death, each of us leaves our mark on the world through our own particular sequence of life events. These may vary from the commonplace, such as marriage, employment, and social or recreational achievements, to the less common events that might give some individuals added interest. Polly Button's family tree would appear to be no different to any other family tree in this regard: for example, within more than 2,100 direct descendants traced, there were instances of particular consequence or notoriety interspersed among the more routine findings. These included convictions for various misdemeanours, a suicide, another murder victim and at least two descendants achieving fame through their work on television or in the theatre.

Although still concentrated in the Midlands to a large extent, especially Leicester, Nuneaton and Walsall, descendants were found to have spread far and wide over the years, with branches now established in the USA and Australia. As the concluding section to this retelling of Polly Button's story, it is hoped that insight into the consequent life stories of her children and brief details of a small selection of noteworthy descendants will be of interest and may provide inspiration to delve more deeply into one's own family history. You never know what you might find!

Elizabeth Green – b. 15 June 1814

Polly Button's eldest child, Elizabeth, married within two years of her mother's murder. The events surrounding her marriage are of some interest. The first of the three scheduled readings of the banns of her marriage to Thomas Ward took place at St Nicolas Church, Nuneaton, on 3 November 1833. However, the second reading the following week was stopped on the intervention of Thomas's father who objected to the marriage on the grounds of Thomas being underage. Those wishing to marry at this time, if they were under 21 years old, needed the permission of parents. The couple must have been desperate to be together, as records indicate that Elizabeth and Thomas pressed ahead with their plan to marry nevertheless. They headed for the village of Astley, some five miles distant, where their marriage banns were read out in the parish church of St Mary on 17 November, 24 November and 3 December 1833 and where they were married on Monday 23 December 1833.

Elizabeth and Thomas were to raise eight children. They initially lived in Abbey Street, Nuneaton, but moved to Coton Road, Chilvers Coton, sometime between 1841 and 1851. Elizabeth continued to work as a silk weaver until her later years, being listed as a housekeeper in 1891. Thomas worked as a general labourer for most of his life, barring a spell as a canal boatman around 1851, probably at the Canal Wharf, Chilvers Coton. This period of work on the canals looks to have inspired at least one of their children to take up canal boating and given rise to a subsequent generational, occupational interest in canals. Thomas died in March 1891. At some stage in the following ten years, Elizabeth went to live with her son, George, at 22 Mornington Street in Leicester, where, according to her death certificate, she died 'of old age' on 27 February 1901; she was 86 years old. She was buried at Leicester's Welford Road Cemetery on 4 March 1901 in Consecrated Section N, Plot 687.

FROM THE DESCENDANTS OF ELIZABETH GREEN:

Ernest George Sewell (1907–1913) was Polly Button's 2nd great-grandson. On the afternoon of Saturday 4 October 1913, young Ernest had been given ½d by his mother and had gone out for a walk along the Grand Union Canal by Abbey Park Road in Leicester, with his friend, seven-year old Nellie Thornton. His hat had blown off into the water and, in trying to retrieve it, he had fallen into the canal. Unable to effect a rescue, Nellie had run off to seek help. Unfortunately, Ernest had been unable to clamber to safety onto the bank of the canal and had subsequently drowned.[109]

Mary Elizabeth Ward (1905–1994) was Polly Button's 2nd great-grandaughter. Mary was born on 25 April 1905 in Brentford, Middlesex, into the canal boating family of Philip and Hannah Ward. In 1941, Mary became captain of the steam narrowboat, *President*. Both Mary Ward and *President* are now prominently featured at the Black Country Living Museum, Tipton Road, Dudley, and online in the museum's Learning Zone.[110]

William Henry Horobin (1894–1915) was Polly Button's great-grandson. William enlisted in Nuneaton on 1 September 1914 and disembarked at Rouen on 13 May 1915 in the First Battalion of the Dorsetshire Regiment, part of the 15th Brigade

109 *Leicester Daily Post*, 8 October 1913, p. 4.
110 https://www.bclm.co.uk/learning/mary-ward/1077.htm

in the Fifth Division. He was to be killed in action on Hill 60, Zillebeke, near Ypres, less than two months later. Hill 60, so called because it was 60 feet above sea level, was a slight prominence that provided an advantageous position to whoever held it, as it gave a clear view to Ypres over the frontline positions. Hill 60 formed a sharp and pronounced projection (salient) into the German lines, so the British soldiers who fought to capture and hold it were open to attack on three sides. As the German artillery was very greatly superior both in number and calibre, holding the position proved to be extremely costly.[111] Between 3pm and 6pm on Monday 5 July 1915, British positions on the hill were subject to a relentless and violent bombardment with minenwerfer (short range mortars) and field gun shells. William had been stationed in Trench 38 and was one of 23 British soldiers killed in the bombing that afternoon.[112] He is buried in nearby Larch Wood (Railway Cutting) Cemetery, grave II.J.15.

Ernest Thomas Ison (1898–1915) was Polly Button's 2nd great-grandson. A private in the Royal Warwickshire Regiment (2nd Battalion), Ernest arrived in France on 18 May 1915. He was killed in action in the Battle of Loos on Saturday 25 September 1915, just two weeks after his 17th birthday. He is remembered on Panel 22–25 of the Loos Memorial.

Henry Ison (1877–1916) was Polly Button's great-grandson. A coal miner by occupation, Henry arrived in France on 31 July 1915 with the Royal Warwickshire Regiment (11th Battalion). He was killed the following year, on 15 November 1916, in the Somme Offensive, just three days before the end of the 4½ month-long battle. He is remembered on Pier 9 of the Thiepval Memorial.

Henry Tonks (1896–1918) was Polly Button's great-grandson. Henry enlisted on 2 September 1914 and arrived in France in May 1915 with the 1st Battalion of the Dorsetshire Regiment. He was killed on 4 June 1918, aged 22, in the Battle of the Avre, the Second Battle of the Somme. He is buried at Berles New Military Cemetery, Pas de Calais (Grave ll. B. 7).

---

111 Hussey and Inman, p. 73.
112 First Battalion Dorsetshire Regiment War Diary, The National Archives, Kew. WO/1572/2.

William Green – b. 15 January 1818

On 16 August 1834, when sixteen years old and some two and a half years after his mother had been murdered, William was apprenticed to William Russell, a bit and snaffle maker, of Walsall, Staffordshire. The apprenticeship indenture document[113] required William to live with Russell and serve him in his apprenticeship until he was twenty-one years old. In return, Russell was to '*teach and instruct, or cause to be taught and instructed, in the best way and manner that he can*' the skills of a bit and snaffle maker. A snaffle bit is perhaps the most common type of bit used when riding horses, consisting of a straight or jointed mouthpiece with rings on each end which connect to reins.

In comparison with Nuneaton, Walsall offered many potential advantages for young William. In the decade or so prior to his apprenticeship, Walsall had '*been greatly enlarged and improved by the formation of new streets, the improvement of old ones, and the erection of a considerable number of very handsome houses, villas, and public buildings; so that it now ranks as the second manufacturing town in the county... and yields to none of them in beauty and elegance.*'[114] Its population had increased by almost 50% in the first thirty years of the nineteenth century, in 1834 standing at 15,066. This compares with the drop in Nuneaton's population in the 1830s and its widespread poverty, destitution and dreadful standards of public health.

Whereas one might see Nuneaton, with its dependence on silk weaving, as a 'one-trick pony', Walsall had a very dynamic and broadly-based expanding economy centred mainly on metal-working, particularly the manufacture of small articles in iron and brass. It had specialised in the manufacture of the metal parts of saddlery and the number of such works had expanded rapidly in the early nineteenth century, so that by 1834 there were 144 bit-makers alone. Although the trade was initially concentrated in Bloxwich, many bit and stirrup workshops had been established in the centre of Walsall itself, including Blue Lane. William

---

113 Warwickshire Record Office, Parish of St Nicolas, Overseers of the Poor Law, Apprenticeship Indentures DR280/85/25B.

114 White, p. 415.

Russell, snaffle (bit) maker, is listed in 1834 as occupying Bagnall's Buildings, Blue Lane[115] and in the 1841 Census as still living in Blue Lane, Walsall, so it seems likely that this is where William would have lived and served his apprenticeship. In 1839, having successfully completed his five years with Russell, William went to work for Job Craddock as a journeyman snaffle maker and is listed in the 1841 Census as living in Craddock's household at Garden Walk, Walsall Foreign.

In March 1851, William was living in Red Lion Street, Walsall, and still working as a snaffle bit maker. Later that year, on 22 September 1851, he married Susannah Reynolds at St Peter's Church, Walsall. All seemed to have been set fair for William and Susannah to build a family life together but, unfortunately, this did not prove to be the case. Tragedy was to strike. In the summer of 1853, Susannah gave birth to twin girls – Mary and Barbara – who were baptised on 19 August 1853 in St Peter's Church, Walsall. The girls were named after the couple's mothers. Tragically, both babies were to die just over two weeks later on 4 September. The next we see of William and Susannah is in the 1861 Census, living in Railway Street, Walsall. There are no others in the household, so we must assume that they had no more children or that if they did the children did not survive to 1861. William's occupation is listed as a snaffle bit filer. Then a second life tragedy befell William, when Susannah died suddenly following a brain haemorrhage or stroke on 27 March 1864 when only 35 years old. The couple's circumstances must have deteriorated rapidly prior to this, as on Susannah's death certificate William is recorded as a pauper. Left grieving the loss of his wife and probably in poor financial circumstances, William died just over two months later, suffering from kidney disease, on 2 June 1864 at the Union Workhouse, Pleck Road, Walsall. He was 46 years old. There would be no children to carry on the Green family name through Polly Button's only son. He was buried on 4 June 1864 at the Queen Street Cemetery, Walsall, in Area D/Section 6/Grave 60.

---

115 Ibid., p. 435.

Hannah Green – b. 5 March 1820

Hannah married James Horobin in St Nicolas Church, Nuneaton on 3 March 1839, just two days short of her nineteenth birthday. Their first child, James, was born in the autumn of the same year. Between 1839 and 1862 the couple had a further five boys and three girls, with all but two living to adulthood. James had been a silk weaver from Chilvers Coton, and the couple continued to work as silk weavers, firstly in Abbey Street, Nuneaton (1841) and then in Coton Road, Chilvers Coton, until at least 1861. After James died of scrofula tuberculosis of the neck on 24 September 1862, Hannah moved back to Abbey Street, Nuneaton, with her remaining family. In 1871, Hannah and five of her children are recorded as living in Abbey Street, Nuneaton, with all but one (Albert) working as silk weavers. As the silk trade continued to decline in Nuneaton, so did Hannah's employment. In 1881 she was unemployed and living with her son Arthur, a 22-year-old railway labourer, at 19 Court, Abbey Street. Hannah died suffering from bronchitis on 25 March 1890, survived by six of her children. She was buried on 29 March 1890 in grave number 96 (General) in Oaston Road Cemetery, Nuneaton. She had lived in Nuneaton and Chilvers Coton all her life, the only one of Polly Button's children to do so.

FROM THE DESCENDANTS OF HANNAH GREEN:

Arthur Horobin (1895–1918). Arthur was Polly Button's great-grandson. He was born on 10 March 1895, the 10th of 12 children born to Albert and Ann Horobin. Arthur was an infantryman in the 1/8th Battalion of the Royal Warwickshire Regiment, part of the 75th Brigade in the 25th Division of the 4th Army that took part in the Second Battle of the Sambre on 4 November 1918. This was the last large-scale, set-piece battle fought by the British Expeditionary Force on the Western Front, similar in scale to the first day of the Battle of the Somme, and took place just one week before the Armistice. The battle was a concerted attack on the German position at Landrecies, France, where the initial task of the Division was to advance 1.5 miles on a 2,000-yard front up to the Sambre Canal. The canal, 53–55 feet wide and more than six feet deep, then had to be crossed and the town of Landrecies entered and taken.[116] Battle had commenced with a main barrage from the British at Zero Hour, 06.15. The 1/8th Royal Warwickshire advanced in front of No. 3 Bridging Party *'over very difficult terrain'* (a dense patchwork of small fields containing orchards, separated by thick hedges) and through the well-defended village of Faubourg Soyeres, their objective being *'to bridge the canal between the Lock and the left Divisional Boundary'* and secure the bridgehead on the canal.[117] However, it was a foggy day and many hostile machine-gun nests were missed by the advancing troops.[118] Given the difficulties and obstacles faced by the regiment in the attack, there were surprisingly few (22) soldiers killed.[119] Unfortunately, Arthur was one of them. He was subsequently buried in the Landrecies British Cemetery (plot B25). Wilfred Owen, the great war poet, was also killed in action that day in the same attack, about two miles distant. A play about Arthur Horobin's war experience, *The Boy from the Boro*, was researched and written by Roger Price and Stuart Horobin (no known relation). Stuart Horobin first performed the role of Arthur Horobin at the Blue Orange Theatre in Birmingham on 11 July 2014 as part of the Birmingham Fest (see Figure 40). Between 2014 and 2018, and in commemoration of the First World War Centenary, the play was performed on 13 occasions at venues throughout the Midlands.

Fig. 40.
Arthur Horobin (1895–1918). I laid the wreath shown in the central image at Arthur Horobin's grave on 4 November 2018 in commemoration of the 100th anniversary of his death.

116 Williams, p. 160.
117 Clayton, p. 173; Williams, p. 161.
118 Undated correspondence from the Royal Regiment of Fusiliers Museum (Royal Warwickshire); Clayton, p. 234.
119 Clayton, p. 179.

Kirk Lee T Bevins (1986-) is Polly Button's 4th great-grandson. Kirk Bevins was the winner of Series 60 of the long-running daytime show, Countdown, achieving the first ever perfect game in the 15-round format on 4 March 2009. He achieved his second perfect score in the show's 30th Birthday Championships in 2013. He is also one of four darts referees on the Professional Darts Corporation (PDC) circuit.

Ann Green – b. 30 January 1826

There are no records to indicate what happened to Ann immediately after her mother had been murdered, although it probably involved some intervention from the Poor Law guardians, as in 1841 when aged 15 she is recorded as living at the Nuneaton workhouse in College Street, Chilvers Coton. She was not to remain there long, for on 16 January 1842 she married Nathaniel Kelsey, a ribbon weaver from Back Lane, Nuneaton. Fast forward almost twenty years and in 1861 we find the couple at 2 Matthews Buildings in King Street, Spitalfields, London, with their four children. Harriet, the eldest child, had been born within a few months of Hannah and Nathaniel marrying and had been baptised on 10 July 1842 in Nuneaton. It would seem that the couple may have delayed having further children until they had relocated to the Spitalfields area, as their last three children are all recorded as being born in Bethnal Green.

Spitalfields had been a centre for silk weaving since the fifteenth century, a position that had been strengthened with the arrival of Huguenot refugees after the revocation of the Edict of Nantes in 1685. However, the 1824 Act repealing the prohibition on the importation of foreign silk had marked the start of a terminal decline in silk weaving in this country. We have already seen the devastation that had been wrought on Britain's silk weaving communities, including Nuneaton, in the years following the introduction of the 1824 Act. The Spitalfields/Bethnal Green area had been particularly badly affected by the repeal of prohibition and had continued on a downward spiral in the following decades. In 1824 there had been approximately 25,000 looms in the area and at least 50,000 people directly dependent on the trade. However, the 1824 Act and a further reduction in the import tariff on silk goods from 30% to 15% in 1846 wreaked such havoc in Bethnal Green that by 1860 there were only 9,500 people working in the trade. The introduction of free trade with France under the Cobden–Chevalier Treaty in January 1860 was to mark the beginning of the end of silk weaving in London: by 1880 only 3,300 people were employed in the trade, and by the time of the 1901 Census a mere 548 people remained working in silk weaving.

While one can hypothesise about the motivation for Ann and Nathaniel Kelsey moving away from Nuneaton to London's Bethnal Green at some stage in the period 1841 to 1853, we will probably never know for sure what their reasons were. It may have been that, having exhausted their local job prospects and having experienced the dreadful conditions that had arisen in their home town, they decided to take their silk weaving skills to London and take their chances in the capital. It is likely that as skilled, male hand-loom weavers were thrown out of work in northern and central England and were increasingly replaced by machines – often tended by women – many of them went on the move looking for work. Indeed, there are other people from Nuneaton listed in census returns as being resident in Bethnal Green in this period, although it does seem that the allure of the area diminished between 1851 (26 people from Nuneaton resident) and 1861 (14 people from Nuneaton resident). The Kelseys had a neighbour in Matthews Buildings who also came from Nuneaton, a Samuel Merry who lived at 6 Matthews Buildings. He had been born in 1822 in Bond Street Nuneaton, quite near to Back Lane, and so might have been a neighbour or friend of Nathaniel. It could have been the case that the two friends made the decision to seek their fortunes together in London.

The fact remains that the family was living in Spitalfields/Bethnal Green from at least 1853 onwards, in conditions that unfortunately must have mirrored, or even been worse than, those of Nuneaton's darkest days in 1832. A detailed report on the living conditions in Bethnal Green was published by Dr Hector Gavin, a physician and sanitarian in 1848. Terms used most often by Gavin in his report to describe most of the parish include dirt/dirty (71), 'filthy' (37), 'offensive' (25), damp (18), 'disgusting' (11) and fetid

(10). Over the next thirty years or so it would therefore seem likely that the family dwelt in quite awful conditions. King Street, where the family was living in 1861 and 1871, was described by Gavin as *'having conditions destructive of all personal cleanliness and comfort, subversive of moral energy and dangerous to health'*.[120] Similarly, Gavin wrote that Fleet Street, home to Ann Kelsey in 1881, was *'abominably filthy, the gutters are full and partly cover the street with foetid, black, slimy mud; garbage is frequently thrown over its surface; its houses are elevated, consisting of several flats, with different families in each; the ventilation of the rooms is most imperfect, and the smell from them most disagreeable. It will be observed that fever and the other epidemics are rife in this dirty place.'*[121] Bethnal Green was an area of extreme environmental degradation and poverty, with one analysis placing the area as the second poorest London parish in 1841, and the poorest by 1871.[122]

It was to be in this harsh and unpromising setting that Ann and Nathaniel Kelsey raised their family. They continued to work in the silk trade, first as silk fringe weavers (1861), then as trimming weavers (1871). They were to have a total of four children: Harriet (1842), John (1853), George (1857), and Matilda (1858). Evidence suggests that the family's situation remained difficult for many years – daughter Harriet gave birth to her first child (Eliza) in the Wapping Workhouse in 1861, was admitted to that workhouse on three further occasions in 1862, and was recorded as being in the St Leonard's Street workhouse in Bromley-by-Bow in August 1880 with the reason for admittance being recorded as 'abortion'. After the death of her husband in the 1870s, Ann continued to work with silk as a 'fancy weaver', as did her daughter Matilda, and is recorded in the 1881 Census as living in Fleet Street, Bethnal Green. Ann died just a couple of days short of her 61st birthday on 28 January 1887 in St Bartholomew's Hospital in London from ovarian cancer and exhaustion, her address at that time being recorded as 8 Pedley Street, Brick Lane.

---

120 Gavin, p. 11.
121 Ibid., p. 37.
122 Green, pp. 118–119.

FROM THE DESCENDANTS OF ANN GREEN:

Ethelbert Frederick Doubleday (1890–1908) was Polly Button's 2nd great-grandson. Following a conviction for robbing his father, Ethelbert was sentenced to 12 months imprisonment. However, while incarcerated at Wormwood Scrubs the somewhat morose and uncommunicative eighteen-year-old was to commit suicide by hanging himself using his handkerchief and part of his sheet.[123]

    Thomas Aldridge (1982-) is Polly Button's 5th great-grandson and is an English television and theatre actor. He has appeared in TV series such as *Silent Witness* and *Call the Midwife*, and his extensive theatrical CV includes *Les Misérables*, *High Society* and *His Dark Materials*. Most recently, he has been playing the character of Ron Weasley in *Harry Potter and the Cursed Child* in London's West End.[124]

Jane Green – b. 21 Sep 1829

The last of three children fathered by John Danks (the first two were from his first marriage, to Sarah Ward), Jane Green is recorded in the 1841 Census as being in the household of Ann Savage, a ribbon weaver living in Abbey Street. As a two-year-old girl at the time of her mother's murder it would appear likely that she had been taken in by a neighbour, with or without a direction from the local Poor Law guardians. A decade later, Jane is listed as a ribbon weaver in the household of John Taylor in Garretts Lane, Attleborough. On 7 December 1851, Jane married widower Joseph Lilley, a ribbon weaver from Attleborough, in Nuneaton's St Nicolas Parish Church and their first child, Mary Ann, was born in the early summer of 1854. The family soon moved the thirty or so miles to Walsall in Staffordshire, where their next child, Susannah (possibly named after her brother William's wife) was born in late 1856. Their third and final child, Clara, followed in 1859. The couple were to remain in Walsall for the rest of their lives, with Joseph finding work as a miner. It seems probable that the couple moved to Walsall so that

---

123 *Tower Hamlets Independent and East End Local Advertiser*, 10 October 1908, p. 4.

124 https://www.imdb.com/name/nm2437026/

Jane could be close to her brother William and his wife Susannah, following the death of their baby twin girls in 1853, as their first recorded address in Walsall (1861 Census) was Holden's Court in Portland Street, only a couple of hundred yards away from where William and Susannah were living in Railway Street. By 1881, Jane and Joseph had fallen on hard times, being recorded as being on 'parish pay' at their home in Birchills, Walsall. Joseph died in 1893 but Jane survived another ten years before dying of senile decay on 30 March 1903 at 2 Court, Short Acre Street, Walsall. She was buried at Ryecroft Cemetery on 4 April 1903, her burial plot location being Division 14/Section 5/Grave 128.

FROM THE DESCENDANTS OF JANE GREEN:

Valerie A Brotherton (1938–1962). Valerie Brotherton, Polly Button's 3rd great-grandaughter, was the second of two daughters born to Bernard and Doris Brotherton when living in Musgrave Road, Birmingham. In November 1958, when quite advanced in pregnancy, she married a 36-year-old lorry driver named Joseph Nathaniel Barrow. Their son was born one month later. However, the marriage was not a happy one and the couple separated. Valerie then lived at various addresses in Birmingham and it was at one of these, in Cranemore Street, Nechells, that she was murdered, by strangulation, on 20 November 1962. Her husband was arrested and tried for the murder. He was found guilty on 5 March 1963 and sentenced to life imprisonment.[125]

As can be seen from this short selection of some of Polly Button's descendants, research into Polly Button's family tree has shown it to be perhaps typical of most if not all family trees, comprising individuals whose lives appear to span a wide range of human existence and experience.

---

125 *Birmingham Daily Post* 6 March 1963, p. 7.

POLLY BUTTON REVEALED: JOURNEY'S END

Uncovering the background to Polly Button's tragic life and bloody murder has been a fascinating journey over the last few years. From an initial interest in establishing the general circumstances surrounding the murder, my researches broadened to include, necessarily, the awful scale of the problems she faced as she struggled to raise her family in a period of prolonged poverty and destitution in Nuneaton. The weakness in the town's economy (a singular dependence on silk ribbon weaving) was a critical factor in the depth and duration of the depression that overwhelmed the town in the years around 1832. The consequences of a manufacturing class that had not invested in technological innovation nor developed the education, skills and training of workers, meant that many in the community were severely affected by the bitter winds of industrialisation and free trade that swept the country in the post-Napoleonic era.

As with many women of this period in similarly precarious and low paid occupations, it is likely that Polly Button may have needed to resort to occasional prostitution to provide for her family, although we cannot be certain of the nature or extent of such actions. Her heroic efforts to return to her family after Danks had launched his vicious attack were an incredible demonstration of human strength, resilience and 'life force'.

If we take 1813 as the high point in her life – living in the big purl time in Nuneaton, pregnant for the first time and with a future that might have appeared full of optimism and hope –

we can see that her life followed an inexorable downward path to her bloody and lonely death on a footpath one cold Saturday night in February 1832. The survival of all of her five children to adulthood is testament to her maternal qualities. As more and more descendants become aware of their shared ancestral link to Polly Button, it is fervently hoped that the story of Polly Button will continue to be disseminated – long may the ripples continue!

UNDOING POLLY BUTTON –
THE ANNEXES

ANNEXE 1: POLLY BUTTON – PROSTITUTE?

Introduction

While prostitution, per se, has never been illegal in the UK, an issue that arose in court during John Danks's trial was the character and status of Polly Button. In general terms, newspaper coverage of the murder and subsequent trial had been unflattering in its descriptions of her. Although they suggested a questionable morality, for example through the use of the term 'indiscriminate intercourse', only one newspaper reference has been found that explicitly referred to her as a prostitute. Commentators have repeatedly noted the difficulty, if not impossibility, of establishing the scale of prostitution in Great Britain throughout the nineteenth century.[126] To help gauge and compare the extent of prostitution in any area in the mid-nineteenth century, however, Mayhew suggested using the proportion of illegitimate births as a proxy indicator for the level of prostitution. Illegitimacy had slowly risen from 3% in about 1750 to around 7% in the 1840s.[127] In the 1840s, the period analysed by Mayhew, Warwickshire had

---

126 Royden, p. 5; Tait, p. 121; Walkowitz, p. 14.
127 https://www.familysearch.org/wiki/en/Illegitimacy_in_England, accessed 11 March 2018.

an average illegitimacy rate of 56 illegitimate births per 1,000 total births (5.6%), comparing well with the national average of 6.7% and placing Warwickshire in the 'top' quartile of counties (34th out of 42).[128] An analysis of the 4,675 records in the parish register of baptisms for St Nicolas Parish Church for the years 1814–32 (from the birth of Polly Button's first child, Elizabeth, to the year of Polly Button's murder) indicates an illegitimacy rate in Nuneaton that varied between 3.3% and 11.1%, with an average of 7.1%. If one accepts Mayhew's use of illegitimacy as a proxy indicator for the level of prostitution in an area, it therefore appears that Nuneaton had a rate of prostitution higher than the national average and higher than the average for Warwickshire.

In researching the issue of prostitution in this period, use has been made of reference materials that began to be produced from the mid-nineteenth century onwards as an outpouring of concern about the social consequences and dislocations arising from rapid industrialisation and urbanisation. Many of these were penned by self-styled experts, including moral, temperance and religious campaigners. In addition, writers with medical and public health backgrounds were also looking to identify ways to address 'The Great Social Evil'.

The publications were often very expansive in their consideration of the many facets of prostitution. Now we have a clearer picture of the life and times of Polly Button and Nuneaton in the first three decades of the nineteenth century (see Chapter 3 – 'Hungry Heart' and Chapter 4 – 'Badlands'), if we are to make some observations and comments about Polly Button and the choices or options available to her it is perhaps to the causes of prostitution that we should now turn.

Causes of Prostitution – as Proposed by Leading Researchers and Authors on the Subject

Authors came up with various ways to list and classify the causes of prostitution. Frequently referenced authors on prostitution in the nineteenth century and early twentieth century are detailed below,

---

128 Mayhew, p. 469.

together with summaries of their categorisation of the causes of prostitution. While a number of these causes could have led Polly Button towards prostitution, only those causes with a likelihood or corroborating evidence of relevance to her have been highlighted in bold. These factors will then be considered.

WILLIAM TAIT, SURGEON[129]

Natural Causes: Licentious inclination; irritability of temper; pride and love of dress; dishonesty and desire of property; indolence.

Accidental Causes: **Seduction**; inconsiderate and ill-assorted marriages; **inadequate remuneration for needle and other kinds of work in which females are employed**; **want of employment**; intemperance; **poverty**; want of proper surveillance of servants by their masters and mistresses; **ignorance or defective education and religious instruction**; bad example of parents; attendance on evening dancing schools and dancing parties; theatre going; desecration of the Sabbath; the publication of improper works and obscene prints; the countenance and reward which is given to vice, and the small encouragement to virtue.

WILLIAM LOGAN, SCOTTISH MISSIONARY AND TEMPERANCE CAMPAIGNER[130] (SON OF A WEAVER, COINCIDENTALLY)

1. One fourth from being servants in taverns and public houses, where they had been seduced by men frequenting these places of dissipation and temptation.
2. One fourth from the intermixture of the sexes in factories, and those employed in warehouses, shops, etc.
3. One fourth by procuresses, or females, who visited country towns, markets and places of worship, for the purpose of decoying good-looking girls.
4. The remaining fourth could be divided into three classes – firstly, those who were indolent or possessed bad tempers and who left their situations; secondly, **those who were**

---

129 Tait.
130 Logan.

**driven to such an awful course by young men making
false promises**; thirdly, those children who have been urged
by their mothers to become prostitutes for a livelihood.

HENRY MAYHEW AND BRACEBRIDGE HEMYNG[131]

Mayhew was a social researcher and journalist who compiled an
extensive series of newspaper articles he had written into a three-
volume book series *London Labour and the London Poor* (1851), a
groundbreaking and influential survey of the city's poor. A fourth
volume, *Those That Will Not Work*, was added in 1861, covering
prostitutes, swindlers, thieves and beggars. Of local note and interest
with regard to this final volume, the sixty or so pages on prostitution
in London were written by (Samuel) Bracebridge Hemyng (b. 1841).
Bracebridge Hemyng was the eldest son of Dempster Heming,
lawyer, of Caldecote Hall, Warwickshire, who is thought to have
been the inspiration for the character of Harold Transome in *Felix
Holt, the Radical* by George Eliot. Quite how Bracebridge Hemyng
came to be qualified to write so extensively about prostitution in
the capital when aged only twenty years old and fresh out of Eton
remains a puzzle. The fact that Hemyng went on to write the highly
successful Jack Harkaway adventure series of 'penny dreadfuls'
comprising gory tales and wholesome escapades perhaps indicates
some useful and significant imaginative and journalistic attributes.

Hemyng acknowledged there were many causes to account for
what he termed 'clandestine prostitutes', a sub-category of which
he identified as 'female operatives' (women from a number of
trades including millinery, silk winding and dress making), where
the following were given as the main causes of such operatives
swelling the ranks of prostitution:

1. **Low wages inadequate to their sustenance.**
2. Natural levity and the example around them.
3. Love of dress and display, coupled with the desire for a
    sweetheart.

---

131 Mayhew.

4. **Sedentary employment and want of proper exercise.**
5. Low and cheap literature of an immoral tendency.
6. Absence of parental care and the inculcation of proper precepts. In short, bad upbringing.

AGNES MAUDE ROYDEN, PREACHER AND SUFFRAGIST[132]

Royden analysed 669 case histories of prostitutes and attributed 40% of the causes of entry into prostitution to 'Tastes and Temperament' as follows: vanity; love of pleasure; an adventurous spirit; bad companions; a wilful and uncontrollable nature; laziness; love of sweets; obligation to pay bridge debts; strongly developed sexual inclinations; deliberate choice with a view to profits. Under this heading, Royden also made linkages to: amusements (theatre, dancing-halls, etc.); dress (good clothes and finery); **(the presence/ involvement of)** soldier, sailor, and **gentleman**.

The remaining 60% of causes identified in the analysis were: bad homes and the desecration of childhood; homelessness; unhappy homes; orphans; temporary homelessness; **seduction and desertion**; compulsion and exploitation; feeble-mindedness/ mental deficiency; natural propensity (strong sexual appetites).

Commentary

From the various analyses and categorisation of the causes of prostitution that have been given above, it would appear that the main influencing factors on Polly Button's decisions with regard to prostitution might have been two-fold. Firstly, that her first pregnancy could have been the result of seduction (by Daniel Wagstaff Jnr) and, secondly, that the generally poor – and at times dreadful – economic conditions in the silk ribbon weaving industry in Nuneaton drove her to prostitution as the only available means to provide for herself and children. These two main, specific influencing factors are now considered below.

---

132 Royden.

1. SEDUCTION

The father of Polly Button's first child, Daniel Wagstaff Jnr, was from a well-to-do family and the relationship with Polly Button may well have been that of a young man 'sowing his wild oats'. The nature of the relationship between the couple, and Polly's belief in where it might lead, must include the possibility of seduction or deception on the part of Wagstaff. The long-term consequences for Polly Button will almost certainly have been detrimental, as being an unmarried mother with a young child would probably have damaged her reputation and led to subsequent difficulties in finding a suitable and stable partner. The following quotation by Timothy Dwight will be seen as quite damning of the likes of Wagstaff, should seduction have been at the root of his actions. It might also provide insight into the psychological consequences for Polly Button.

> *Seduction, in its very nature, involves fraud of the worst kind. It is probably always accomplished by means of the most solemn promises, and often with oaths still more solemn. Both the promises and oaths, however, are violated in a manner supremely profligate and shameful. The object to which they are directed is base, malignant, and treacherous in the extreme; and the manner in which it is prosecuted is marked with the same treachery and baseness. He who can coolly adopt it has put off the character of a man, and put on that of a fiend; and with the spirit of a fiend alone, he pursues and accomplishes the infernal purpose. The ruin sought and achieved is immense. It is not the filching of property. It is not the burning of a house. It is not the deprivation of liberty. It is not the destruction of life. The seducer plunders the wretched victim of character, morals, happiness, hope and heaven; enthrals her in the eternal bondage of sin, consumes her beyond the grave in endless fire; and murders her soul with an ever-living death. All of this is perpetrated under strong professions of peculiar affection, with the persuasive language of tenderness, and with the smiles of gentleness and complacency. For, the seducer 'Can smile, and smile, and be a villain'.* [133]

---

133 Logan, p. 39.

Similarly, Tait makes reference to a class of prostitute consisting of those brought up under a good moral and religious training but, *'in an unguarded moment have allowed themselves to be mis-led by the wiles of an artful seducer, and have been left to hide their shame, at a distance… in a life of profligacy and debauchery.'*[134] Tait later writes that it appears that the active agents (seducers) tend to *'belong to the middle or highest ranks, where their education, wealth and influence should be directed to the promotion of virtue and morality, rather than to rendering themselves conspicuous and powerful as promotors of vice, sorrow and wretchedness. So far as can be determined, about eighteen per cent. of all the common women have become prostitutes in consequence of seduction, and eighty per cent. of all who have been seduced, have been led astray by individuals moving in a higher sphere than themselves.'* Those deserted are left *'to a life of misery, wretchedness, poverty and suffering'.*[135]

In one late nineteenth century survey, almost a fifth of prostitutes (2,386 out of 16,000) gave 'seduction' as the immediate cause for their entering into prostitution; of these almost one quarter said they had been seduced by a 'gentleman', although the term 'gentleman' would appear to have been used in a very wide sense.[136] Royden noted that the histories of girls driven into prostitution by seduction were monotonously similar and suggested that a seduced girl may be so driven by any or all of the following three influences: *'emotional shock consequent on seduction and desertion, the unfavourable effect it had on her economic position, and the loss of character that exposed her to temptation and persecution from unscrupulous persons.'*[137]

2. POVERTY, DESTITUTION AND WANT OF EMPLOYMENT

Walkowitz, writing more recently on the subject of prostitution in the Victorian age, has suggested that most women's entry into prostitution appears to have been circumstantial rather than premeditated, and most likely a response to local conditions of

---

134 Tait, p. 36.
135 Ibid. p. 96.
136 Merrick, p. 40.
137 Royden, pp. 89–90.

the urban job market than anything else. For those placed in a vulnerable economic and social position, some women may have found prostitution a temporary solution to their immediate difficulties.[138] It should be noted that such difficulties were often severe, a predicament that had been the subject of observations by previous commentators. Acton, quoting extensively from interviews Mayhew held with numerous prostitutes, makes for depressing reading:

> *At times I was so badly off, me and my boy, that I was forced to resort to prostitution to keep us from starving. Had the price I was paid for my labour been such that I could get a living by it, I would never have resorted to the streets for money… But the world has drove me about so, and poverty and trouble has forced me to do what I never did before. I do the best I can with what little money I earn, and the rest I am obligated to go to the streets for. My wages will barely find me in food. Indeed, I eat more than I earn, and I am obligated to make up my money in other ways… It was the smallness of the price I got for my labour that drove me into prostitution as a means of living. In my heart I hated it; my whole nature rebelled at it, and nobody but God knows how I struggled to give it up.* [139]

Confirmation of the devastating impact of unemployment, low wages, the seasonality of work and periodic industrial depressions as occurred in Nuneaton in the period during which Polly Button raised her family has also been highlighted by several writers in the field. Tait made the following observations: '*Where one is known to follow a life of prostitution in the less impoverished ranks of society, two or more will be found to do so in the most destitute classes. Destitution appears to be an evil which removes every barrier of restraint, and breaks up all order, and all regard for the laws of morality and religion in the class of society where it is most severely felt.*'[140] He added: '*Women might suffer much themselves from want and oppression before having recourse to immoral means to supply them; but few mothers could long*

---

138 Walkowitz, p. 14.
139 Acton, p. 23–25.
140 Tait, p. 13.

endure to hear the cries of their hungry children, without making sacrifices to which nothing else would cause them to submit.'[141] Royden noted that: '*a woman may earn a good wage for nine months of the year* [although this almost certainly would not have been the case for Polly Button] *and yet be forced into prostitution by economic pressure during the other three months of the year.*' [142] And as regards seasonal fluctuations: '*the wages in* [certain] *occupations are seldom such as would afford a sufficient income if spread over the whole year. There is no doubt that many workers are forced to take to the streets to tide over these lean months. This intermittent prostitution… is very difficult to detect… but from outside observers and from the workers themselves we learn that the seasonal occupation automatically condemns many of its hands to regular periods of prostitution.*'[143]

Walkowitz has also made the point that prostitution was linked to male leisure patterns and therefore responded to fluctuations in trade cycles and economic rhythms.[144] The periodic and extensive silk trade depressions that savaged Nuneaton could therefore have further restricted Polly Button being able to provide for her family through prostitution by reducing her potential client base amongst the unemployed weavers in the town. This could only have made her desperate situation even worse.

Reflecting on the tremendous potential for a lonely and isolated existence, as might well have been the case for Polly Button, Royden also makes the following interesting point: '*They forget that even if a woman's labour brings her food and shelter and clothing, the vital necessity of enjoyment is still lacking and that she will be tempted to buy it with her only other asset, her sexual attraction. The imperative desire for self-realisation by experience of those entrancing pleasures and interests of life… make a wage on the subsistence level very little protection from prostitution.*' [145]

---

141 Ibid., p. 112.
142 Royden, pp. 139 & 142.
143 Ibid., pp. 141–2.
144 Walkowitz, p. 23.
145 Royden, p. 151.

Conclusion – and a Suggested Realistic Scenario

While we will never know for sure if, and to what extent, Polly Button engaged in prostitution, we can produce a realistic scenario based on the available evidence that has been assembled about her life and experience in the harsh conditions that prevailed in Nuneaton between 1815 and 1832. This period in her life can be set against a background of a failure by the church to deliver religious and moral leadership for the town of Nuneaton at a crucial time in its history (see Chapter 4 – 'Badlands'). At the same time, Nuneaton was being exposed to severe economic, social and environmental stresses arising from the rapid industrialisation of the ribbon weaving trade and the opening up of free trade within Europe.

The scenario, therefore, starts with Polly Button being seduced by the well-to-do Daniel Wagstaff Jnr who either had no intention of marrying her, decided that he did not want to marry her, or was prohibited from doing so by his father. This proved to be a fateful outcome for Polly Button. As a single parent with one child to bring up, she may have been seen in an unfavourable light by potential future husbands. Given the periodic and significant depressions in the ribbon weaving trade in Nuneaton, and the town's inability to mount an effective response to the challenges that were arising, Polly Button would not have been able to make a living sufficient for herself and her family. Given the widespread deprivation, poverty and near-starvation that existed for many in Nuneaton, it could have been the case that Polly Button resorted to occasional prostitution as her only available means to provide the bare necessities and sustenance for her family. The rationale for judging her prostitution to have been intermittent is based on the fact that the Justices of the Peace were able to grant filiation orders that declared who had been the fathers of her five children, perhaps something they would not have been able to do if her intercourse had been 'indiscriminate', to quote pejorative descriptions from newspaper reports of the time. The early and untimely death of four of the men, and the residence in Birmingham of the fifth, served only to exacerbate her financial difficulties and most likely further reinforce her need to resort to prostitution.

Support for the framework to this suggested scenario has been given by Levin (referencing Walkowitz), as follows: '*Although poverty appears to have been the main factor for a woman's move into prostitution, most women were not driven to prostitution at the point of actual starvation. Rather, prostitution was another option for supplying the basic necessities. For most working-class women, prostitution was a highly casual and seasonal occupation depending on the financial situation of the woman and the demand that existed for her services.*'[146]

---

146 Levin, p. 3.

ANNEXE 2: THE HISTORICAL BACKGROUND

The historical sources that inform our understanding of the dreadful conditions that arose in Nuneaton in the first 30 years or so of the nineteenth century comprise:

- *The Memorandum Book of Occurrences at Nuneaton* (*The Nuneaton Diary*) – a diary kept by a local resident in the first half of the nineteenth century.
- *Reports of the Committee Appointed to Consider of the Several Petitions Relating to Ribbon Weavers* (1818)
- *Select Committee on the Silk Trade* (1832)
- *Select Committee – Hand-Loom Weavers* (1835)
- *Assistant Hand-Loom Weavers' Commissioners' Report* (1840)
- *General Board of Health Report* (1849)

The Nuneaton Diary

The *Memorandum Book of Occurrences at Nuneaton* (also known as *The Nuneaton Diary*) was a personal record maintained from 1810 until 1845 by John Astley, a grocer with premises in Market Place, Nuneaton.[147] The diary paints an intimate and personal picture of life in the town in the first half of the 19th century. It was originally saved for posterity by Alfred Scrivener (1845–1886), the first editor of the *Nuneaton Observer*, after an old

---

147 Astley, J.

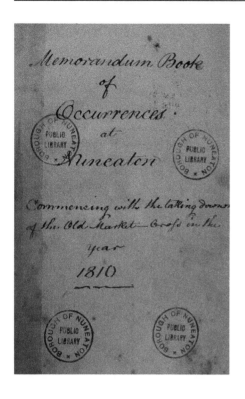

lady walked into his office in Abbey Street and handed over a rather battered notebook which she had discovered in a butcher's shop. She subsequently also presented Scrivener with another section of the diary. Scrivener knew John Astley and identified the diarist straight away, the identification being made easier by the fact that both Alfred's father, Joseph Scrivener, and John Astley were both Inspectors of Nuisances in Nuneaton.

The persistence of poverty and problems within the ribbon weaving trade throughout the first half of the nineteenth century is highlighted by the fact that more than fifty entries in the diary relate to the poor state of the trade and the adverse effect this was having on the town's population. The diary's first mention of problems in the local ribbon weaving industry followed the end of the big purl time when, in late August 1816, it was recorded that a ribbon manufacturer by the name of Hull had been made a bankrupt – the first bankruptcy in the town for more than fifty years. Through the winter months of 1816–17, the diary records the distress of the town increasing – the poor rates more than doubling what they had been six months previously – and relief for the poor being supplemented by £200 and 11 blankets from a charitable society in London.

Although trade picked up from time to time, in November 1822 it was noted that, '*The Ribbon Trade become hard. The weavers not half employed.*' The following winter saw similar conditions in the trade, with September 1823 '*continuing very flat*' and December 1823 being '*particularly bad*'. The diary recorded that the announcement in February 1824 by the Chancellor of the Exchequer that he was proposing to '*take of the Duty on Silk and to addmit Foreign Manufact'd Goods caused considerable uneasiness to the Manufacturers, consider'g it prove of ruinous consequences to the Trade and dependants.*'

Perhaps surprisingly, the summers of the two-year lead-in period for the prohibition (1824 and 1825) proved to be relatively good ones – '*the Ribbon Weavers now in full employ*' (May 1824), '*the Ribbon trade good*' (26 July 1824), '*the Ribbon Trade extraordin'y good. Higher prices given*' (September 1824) and '*the Extraordinary good state of the Ribbon Trade continues unabated. The weavers of Gause Ribbons are receiving very great wages, very few of whom are earning less than a pound a week*' (March 1825). However, any improvement was short-lived.

By December 1825 there had been '*a sudden fall off in the Ribbon Trade*' caused by, according to local manufacturers, '*The Law coming into force in July next admit'g Foreign wrought Silks.*' In January 1826, the ribbon trade was '*depressingly bad*' (for the same given reason). Although noting that the ribbon trade had times of good demand (for example in March 1827), references continued to be made in the diary both to the low prices for weaving and periods of reduced employment (December 1828, February 1829). In 1829, the scale of the depression in the trade became noticeably worse: '*The ribbon trade continues wretchedly bad. The year's Poor Rates am't'd to 5/6 in the pound*' (March 1829); in May 1829, a bankrupt ribbon manufacturer (Hood) from nearby Attleborough absconded to America with debts in the region of £1,200–1,500, and by the summer the trade was in a '*ruinous state*' and '*greatly depressed, a considerable increase in applicants for parochial aid*'.

The desperation to take work at ever lower rates of pay, led to serious social disturbances: '*During the last week the Town was a scene of Riotous Tumult. Various outrages were committed on persons by placing them on an Ass face towards the tail* ['donkeying'] *and conveying them through the Streets for having taken work at low wages. Windows were also broken in several instances and a general Strike for wages ensued*' (28 September 1829). Three weeks later two of the perpetrators of the donkeying were sentenced to two years imprisonment with hard labour at Warwick Crown Court.

November 1829 saw '*the ribbon trade very bad fully participating in the general stagnation of Trade throughout the Country*' and, as there was no improvement in trade, in December '*a Soup Shop established with Bread given to the poor. The soup sold at 1d./Qt. costing ab't 1½, exclusive of the Bread given, having a pound of Meat to the Gallon of Soup.*' The Soup Shop ran until the end of March 1830, at one stage having to increase its distribution to 1,000 gallons a week.

The usual seasonal fall-off in demand for ribbons duly recurred the following winter, with December 1830 seeing '*the ribbon trade flat and many weavers out of employ*' and the Soup Shop reopened again by the Soup Committee.

The cyclical pattern was again repeated in the November of the following year but this time it was accompanied by a significant escalation in the actions of the desperate weavers. The burning down of Josiah Beck's new ribbon weaving factory in Coventry on 7 November 1831 triggered physical attacks in the Nuneaton area on the warehouses, factories and dwellings of three ribbon manufacturers, namely Hood, Clarke and Payne. In a successful attempt to avert other threatened acts of violence, the creation of about 250 Special Constables was funded through a civic subscription '*for watching the town*'. Leading local figures, including Messrs Dugdale, Bracebridge and Newdigate, and the Rev. Samuel Bracebridge Heming, showed their support for the action through their increased presence and 'visibility' in the town. Nuneaton was subsequently patrolled by three nightwatchmen over the winter months.

In November 1831, there was also an enquiry into the scale of unemployment of both looms and people in the town in order to complete a survey that had been sent by the Society for the Relief of Distressed Manufacturers, in London. It revealed that almost three-quarters of the looms lay silent and almost two-thirds of the working population of Nuneaton was consequently unemployed. The collapse in the silk ribbon trade was having a devastating impact on the town.

As 1831 drew to a close, the last entry in the diary for that year makes clear the depth of the crisis that had enveloped the town: '*The year 1831 was a year of great distress to the dependents on the ribbon trade. Ruin and Poverty are the lot of Hundreds in this Town. The Poor Rate doubling, 700 galls Soup given away weekly.*'

Desperate petitions and deputations were organised early in 1832, seeking the return to prohibition of manufactured silk goods and an enquiry into '*the unpresidented distress experienced here by all persons engaged in or dependent on the ribbon trade, attributing such distress mainly caused by the great Importation of Foreign Ribbons since the repeal of the prohibitory Laws which came into operation in 1826.*'

These vivid, personal and very localised entries in Astley's diary were backed up throughout the period it covered by the findings of government-initiated reports, as follows:

REPORTS OF THE COMMITTEE APPOINTED TO CONSIDER OF THE SEVERAL PETITIONS RELATING TO RIBBON WEAVERS (1818)

The distress in the ribbon weaving industry after the ending of the Napoleonic Wars had triggered petitions to Parliament from the communities affected, which included Coventry and Nuneaton. The concerns detailed within the petitions were referred for investigation to a committee of the House of Commons in 1818. The committee heard evidence in March of that year from William Fletcher, a weaver from Nuneaton, that prices were '*extremely low, not affording a maintenance by any means*', and that the poor relief payments to the needy in Nuneaton, with its population of approximately 6,000, had soared between 1815 to 1817 from £3,096 9s 2d to £5,837 4s 2d – an increase of 88.5%.[148] Fletcher confirmed that he had never known the ribbon trade to be in such a state of distress before. On 24 April, the committee received a letter from the inhabitants of Nuneaton and its vicinity, delivered by Mr Paget Taylor, Parish Clerk to Chilvers Coton, who was attending the committee to give evidence. The letter confirmed '*the great distress which prevailed upon the ribbon weavers in the district*' and stated that on 10 February 1817, out of a total of 2,192 looms of both single hand and engine types almost two thirds (1,351) were idle and not in use. The number of inhabitants receiving poor relief had more than doubled from 961 to 2,029 in just a year, with more than a third of the town's population now being relieved.[149]

SELECT COMMITTEE REPORT ON THE SILK TRADE (1832)

Concerns over the consequences of the removal of the prohibition on the importation of silk goods led to the appointment of a select committee to examine what effects the change had produced since

---

148 Committee on Ribbon Weavers (March 1818), pp. 16, 19.
149 Committee on Ribbon Weavers (April/May 1818), p. 129.

1824. Witnesses appearing before the Select Committee on the Silk Trade in 1832 provided unambiguous evidence of the collapse in the wages of those involved in the ribbon trade and the appalling effects that unemployment and poverty had wrought. The report, published in the year of Polly Button's murder, probably provides the most contemporary and accurate account of the parlous state of ribbon weaving communities in Nuneaton and the surrounding area.

In March 1832, Benjamin Poole, a 32-year-old ribbon weaver from Coventry, gave evidence that, '*The condition of the working classes of Coventry is one of the most complete distress; more particularly these last three years; and in my recollection it has never been so great as at the present time, particularly affecting persons in the ribbon trade. A very considerable reduction has taken place in the wages of ribbon weavers since 1826.*'

He confirmed that the engine trade was the prevailing trade in Coventry, so we can deduce that Nuneaton, with its much greater reliance on the less efficient single hand-looms, would have been even more adversely affected. Indeed, the committee put the issue of a greater decrease in wages of the single hand-loom weavers directly to Poole, who acknowledged: '*The rate of wages in a single hand-loom have been most grievously low; so low as not, even with work, to afford a single hand-loom weaver a morsel of bread.*'

Poole suggested that the single hand-loom weaver, in late 1831, may have been earning no more than 2s 6d a week in comparison with the engine-loom weaver's minimum of 7s 6d (which could sometimes reach 12s a week). By extension, therefore, most of Nuneaton's weavers, the overwhelming majority of which worked single hand-looms, may also have been trying to subsist on wages that were only one third of that received by most of Coventry's weavers and which were causing such distress to that group. When employed, Poole estimated that these wages were for working days of 14–16 hours and even, in some parts of the year, up to 18 hours.[150]

Subsequent witnesses from the area also confirmed the scale of the collapse. Edward Goode from Coventry described the city as '*unprecedentedly depressed… want of employment and low wages… a 30% drop in wages since 1819*'. David Smith, a ribbon weaver

---

150 Select Committee on the Silk Trade, pp. 52–4, 60, 62, 68.

from Coventry, asserted that: *'there is very uncertain and irregular employment; consequently, the operatives are very much distressed.'* A weaving undertaker from Foleshill, Joseph Marston, believed that: *'the last two seasons, and more particularly the present, it has been so depressed as I never knew it at this season of the year. It has been on the decline the last four years, but more particularly the last two years.'* Marston estimated weekly earnings at 5s 6d when in full employment, which many were not, and stated that 60% of operatives were without any work whatsoever (1,629 out of 2,691 weavers). Cleophus Ratcliff, a ribbon manufacturer from Coventry, told the committee that he thought, *'There was more distress in the year 1831 than was ever known in Coventry before.'*[151]

Conditions were likely to have been even worse in Nuneaton given its peripheral location to the Coventry trade and its technological and industrial shortcomings. These arose because of the preponderance of the older and less productive single hand-looms, of which Nuneaton had the highest proportion in the area, as shown in Figure 41, using information contained in a later government report, *The Fletcher Report.*

Fig. 41. Number and distribution of single hand-looms in Coventry and Warwickshire silk ribbon weaving communities in 1838. Source: *Fletcher Report 1840,* p. 12.

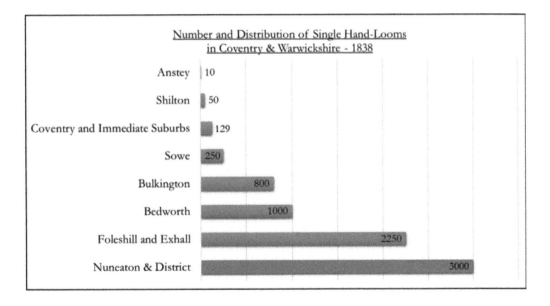

---

151 Select Committee on the Silk Trade, pp. 68, 70, 74, 103, 104.

Inevitably, as the silk weaving industry collapsed, those communities relying on less productive looms for their weaving were to be worse affected. As the end of 1831 approached, the scale of loom redundancy in Nuneaton was the highest in the area and approaching twice that in Coventry (see Figure 47).

Witnesses from other parts of the country vividly conveyed the consequences of the depression on their communities with descriptions of the conditions that were prevailing. Commenting on the general condition of workers since 1826, Barrett Wadden (a silk manufacturer of Spitalfields) thought that it had altered very much for the worse and he considered their condition to be *'wretched in the extreme'* and pointed out to the committee *'the state of degradation and the horrible misery that is inflicted on the working community when I see the wages reduced by 38½ % since 1824'*.[152]

Joseph Grout, a silk goods manufacturer, said there had been a very great change with regard to the morals and character of weavers: *'It is not only the reduction of wages, but we have discharged a great number; some of the men have emigrated, others have gone to the poorhouse; and many of the females have gone, I fear, to a state of prostitution,'* confirming that *'their condition is most abject, and much to be pitied.'*[153] Another witness, Thomas Johnson, a silk thrower, agreed that the operatives were in a very distressed and demoralised condition and said: *'They are sinking fast in a state of degradation; their wants press on them; in various ways, their bellies go half full, their backs half clothed, and the people feel no inclination to send their children to school; and a state of degradation and immorality is fast overtaking them.'*[154]

The committee heard evidence from William Jacombs, a ribbon manufacturer from Nuneaton. He presented an account of the poor rates in the parish of Nuneaton from 1818 to 1832[155] that showed that between 1825 and 1832, the total expenditure on poor relief had more than doubled to stand at £4,782, as shown in Figure 42.

---

152 Select Committee on the Silk Trade, pp. 650–51.
153 Ibid., p. 692.
154 Ibid., p. 807.
155 Ibid., p. 83.

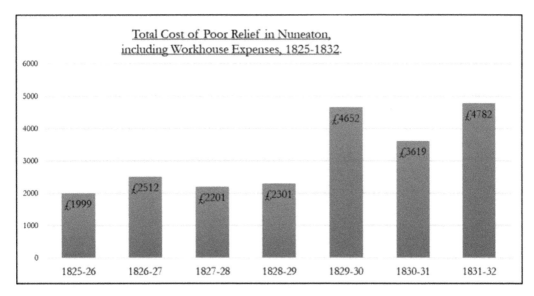

Fig. 42. Total cost of poor relief in Nuneaton 1825–1832. Source: Select Committee on the Silk Trade.

The number of persons receiving poor relief in the same period, besides those in the workhouse, soared from 868 to 3,240, a massive increase of 273% (Figure 43). This dwarfed the increase (111%) that had created significant poverty and destitution in Nuneaton when the silk trade had collapsed just 14 years previously.

Fig. 43. Numbers receiving poor relief in Nuneaton, excluding those in workhouse, 1825–1832. Source: Select Committee on the Silk Trade.

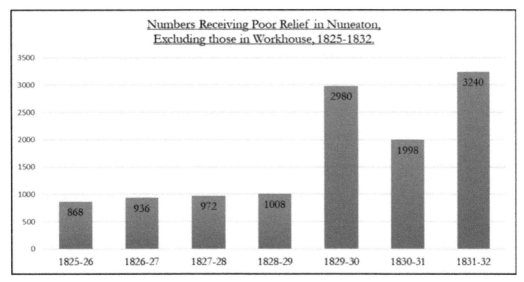

The somewhat puzzling temporary reduction in poor relief in 1830–31 might be accounted for by two pieces of evidence given to the committee by Jacombs. First, he indicated that there had been some slight improvement in trade in 1830.[156] Second, Jacombs had made reference in his evidence to the spirit amongst the poor in the town of keeping themselves out of the poor relief system if they could, even if it meant taking work at less wages than the parish would provide in relief.[157] However, the further collapse of the ribbon trade in the winter of 1831–32 and the abject poverty that resulted served to remove even the fear of public humiliation of being on poor relief. The numbers of those receiving relief and the overall costs of such relief escalated rapidly to unprecedented levels.

Jacombs confirmed that in 1830 soup was given to about 2,500 poor inhabitants, four days each week and that the soup kitchen had been expanded from the middle of November 1831 to cover at least 3,000 inhabitants, almost 40% of the population of the town, including many families who were not receiving parochial relief at all.[158]

He estimated that upwards of 4,000 people were directly involved in the ribbon trade (if they could get employment) and that 6,000 of the town's inhabitants – more than three quarters – were dependent on it.[159] He stated that of the 3,000 looms in the town in December 1831, the greater portion were single hand-looms and confirmed that there had been a very great material reduction in wages since 1826, with many looms having to be sold under duress for less than a quarter of their cost in order to pay rent. It is likely that this situation would have significantly impacted on Danks's ability to make a living from his skills in carpentry through the making or repairing of the wooden single hand-looms, adding to the difficulties he faced.[160]

---

156 Select Committee on the Silk Trade, p. 87.
157 Ibid., p. 93.
158 Ibid., p. 83.
159 Ibid., p. 84.
160 Burwick, p. 128–9

SELECT COMMITTEE REPORT ON HAND-LOOM
WEAVERS' PETITIONS (1835)

Further evidence and insight into the appalling conditions that existed in Nuneaton in the early 1830s as a result of the plight of the hand-loom weavers was given to a select committee set up in 1834 to investigate the concerns that were being raised across the country. Evidence from Charles Hood, a local manufacturer, confirmed that: '*The parish of Nuneaton, owing to the depression among hand-loom weavers in the neighbourhood, is in a very bad state indeed. There are in our parish 3,200 and odd now on the books receiving relief; and the population is 8,000 within a very few*'. He added that: '*Nearly the whole of the population depend on the hand-loom weaving. The shopkeepers and all the persons in all the branches of the trade, and all except the farmers, almost the whole of the population, depend on the trade.*'[161]

Vivid descriptions from witnesses in other towns similarly affected allow us to get an idea of the dire consequences of the collapse in trade and the resultant poverty and squalor in ribbon weaving communities: '*Many of the poor people having very little fire, and no comfortable food or clothing, and especially in the winter, to keep them warm, they get into a reckless condition; they want something to give them comfort, and they think a glass of gin would help them to it, and from that they get habits of drinking. They feel it a degradation; they rather wish to be properly independent, by being justly remunerated for their work. One of the great evils of any class of society becoming impoverished is that it obliterates those feelings of independence, and brings men into a state of degradation, recklessness and vice.*'[162]

A witness from Bolton, a Mr Needham, presented a detailed analysis of the reduction in wages and spending power of hand-loom weavers in his town. As single hand-looms dominated the weaving industry in Bolton, the conditions that existed in that town are likely to have been very similar to those in Nuneaton. In his evidence, Needham evaluated the wages that could have been earned for weaving a standardised number of woven articles averaged over each of the successive seven-year periods between

161 Select Committee – Hand-Loom Weavers (August 1835), p. 4.
162 Select Committee – Hand-Loom Weavers (August 1835), p. 6.

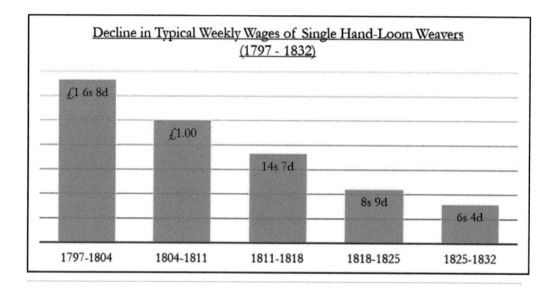

Fig. 44. Decline in typical weekly wages of single hand-loom weavers between 1797 and 1832, based on evidence gathered in Bolton, which had a weaving community and profile very similar to that of Nuneaton. Source: Report of Select Committee on Hand-Loom Weavers' Petitions (August 1835).

1797 and 1832. He had established what quantities of essential foodstuffs could have been bought with the wages that had been so earned by referring to the cost of basic foodstuffs (flour, oatmeal, potatoes and meat) that had been recorded in the town's workhouse records over that period. His conclusion was that between 1797 and 1832 there had been an overall fall in wages of 76%, and an almost commensurate decline (70.6%) in the ability to be able to purchase essential food items from the wages earned – see Figure 44.[163] The consequences for weavers living in towns like Bolton and Nuneaton must have been catastrophic.

David Shaw, a single hand-loom ribbon weaver from Nuneaton, had been selected by the town's weavers to represent them. He gave his evidence in April 1835. Shaw estimated that his wages had collapsed by about two thirds between the early 1800s and 1835 to around 4s 8d.[164] He also confirmed that the vast majority of the fall, perhaps up to 76% of this total reduction, had occurred in the nine years following the removal of prohibition in 1826.[165] This evidence provides confirmation of the speed and depth of the depression that hit Nuneaton in the few years leading up to Polly Button's murder.

---

163 Ibid, pp. 9–10.
164 Select Committee – Hand Loom Weavers (July 1835), pp. 251–52.
165 Ibid., p. 260.

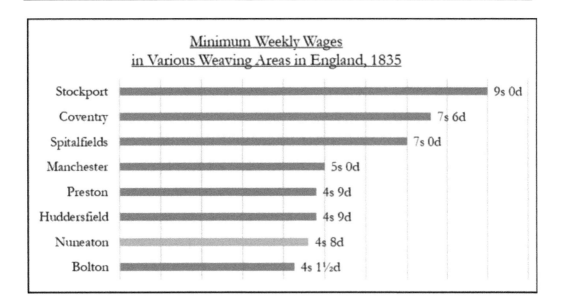

**Minimum Weekly Wages
in Various Weaving Areas in England, 1835**

Area	Wage
Stockport	9s 0d
Coventry	7s 6d
Spitalfields	7s 0d
Manchester	5s 0d
Preston	4s 9d
Huddersfield	4s 9d
Nuneaton	4s 8d
Bolton	4s 1½d

The report, referencing the influential clergyman, theologian and natural philosopher William Paley, confirmed the particular damage that the introduction of power-looms was doing to the livelihood of hand-loom weavers: '*The introduction of the power-loom has been more prejudicial to the hand-loom weavers than to any other class; it has benefited the nation indirectly and injured the population directly. To an individual who has no capital except in his hands, machinery has, like a destroying angel, come and cut off his hands, and permitted the individual to starve by inches. It has been prejudicial to a part of the nation, inasmuch as it has crippled the means of the working population whom it has compelled to work a greater length of time, and to receive less, and all classes to remain longer in business, instead of retiring as they did of old.*'[166]

From evidence put forward to the committee on the average weekly wages for a 'fair average weaver' from 17 towns in England, Scotland and Ireland, Nuneaton's weekly wage rate of 4s 8d was the second lowest of any English town, as shown in Figure 45.[167]

Fig. 45. Minimum weekly wages in various weaving areas in England, 1835. Source: Report of Select Committee on Hand-Loom Weavers' Petitions (July 1835).

---

166 Select Committee – Hand-Loom Weavers (August 1835), p. 19.
167 Select Committee – Hand Loom Weavers (July 1835), p. xii.

It should be noted that although this 'league table' was produced by the committee in its report, some witnesses did provide even more disconcerting figures for earnings. As detailed previously, Benjamin Poole gave a figure of just 2s 6d for the weekly wage for single hand-loom silk ribbon weavers in the Coventry area, while Mr Needham's own evidence to the committee suggested that weavers in Bolton were earning as much as 6s 4d a week. It is certainly possible, therefore, that weavers in Nuneaton were earning less than equivalent weavers in any other part of the country.

David Shaw's evidence on the parlous state of Nuneaton's weavers included his assessment that the state of the hand-loom weavers was '*very miserable indeed. We have a population of 8,000 inhabitants and they are principally dependent, nine-tenths of them, on the silk trade; they are in a state of unutterable distress.*'

He made reference to the last list of agreed prices that had been introduced in Nuneaton, and accepted reluctantly by the weavers, in November 1831. He said that wages had still continued to fall afterwards to some 30% less than the lowest list in many instances.[168] He estimated that his wages were about a third of what they had been for the same number of hours working on the same sort of woven article as they had been 30 years before.[169] Shaw confirmed that he should work very hard to earn the 4s 8d that had been given as the average weekly wage in Nuneaton, working from 13 to 14 hours a day.[170]

Shaw suggested two main influences on the fall of wages: first, the removal of prohibition in 1826 and, second, the lack of more modern and efficient looms. As regards the latter and productive efficiency, he compared the condition of Nuneaton's weavers unfavourably with those in Coventry, confirming that a much greater proportion in Nuneaton were employed in hand-loom weaving, making one ribbon with one shuttle alone, whereas engine-loom weavers could make up to twenty prints in one loom.[171]

Shaw was accompanied by Mr Charles Hood, who followed him in giving evidence. He confirmed that: '*the parish of Nuneaton*

---

168 Select Committee – Hand Loom Weavers (July 1835), p. 250.
169 Ibid., p. 251.
170 Ibid., p. 252.
171 Ibid., p. 260.

is in as bad a state as ever it was in the very worst time… many would be ruined.' He described the very high level of poor relief, the fact that the great dependence of the town on the ribbon weaving was resulting in a widespread depression affecting all descriptions of trade (including shopkeepers, bricklayers and carpenters) and that there were a great many uninhabited houses in the town.[172] This reinforces the finding that Nuneaton, almost uniquely within Warwickshire, suffered a fall in its population in the 1830s as a consequence of the depression that hit the area.

ASSISTANT HAND-LOOM WEAVERS' COMMISSIONERS' REPORT 1840 (FLETCHER REPORT)

Following on from the 1835 Parliamentary select committee reports on petitions from the hand-loom weavers, a Royal Commission on Hand-Loom Weavers was set up in 1837 to enquire into unemployment and poverty in the textile industry and subsequently issued a number of reports between 1839 and 1841. Joseph Fletcher, a statistician and barrister who had been appointed as secretary to the commission, reported on the Midlands in January 1840, with the vast majority of the report focusing on Coventry and the surrounding area, including Nuneaton. The report provides compelling and graphic details of the conditions that prevailed in the weaving communities of Coventry and northern Warwickshire in the 1830s and that would have been all too familiar to Nuneaton's impoverished inhabitants in the winter of 1831–2. Fletcher's report included examinations of the industrial, moral and physical condition of the weavers.

INDUSTRIAL CONDITION

The Report contrasted the slight increases since 1818 in the number of plain engine-looms and single hand-looms with the explosion in the number of Jacquard looms after 1823, introduced to weave fancy ribbons. The ribbon weaving industry was still dominated by Coventry, recorded as having almost 5,000 of the more advanced

---

172 Ibid., p. 263.

plain engine-looms and Jacquard looms (more than 80% of all such looms in the area), whereas Nuneaton had no plain engine-looms and just 200 Jacquard looms present in the town. Nuneaton also paled in comparison when it came to the size and structure of the ribbon trade: Nuneaton had only four ribbon manufacturers compared with the 127 located in Coventry.

By 1838, single hand-looms had virtually disappeared from Coventry and were thereafter mainly to be found in the outlying weaving districts to the north, including (and principally) Nuneaton. It was only here that the undertaking system was maintained, the dispersion of the labour force and its unreliable and frequently untrained nature making necessary some close supervision of the weaving, and mediation between the manufacturer and the weaver. Of the 3,200 looms in Nuneaton, some 3,000 (94%) were single hand-looms, the highest proportion of all the main weaving locations in the area and contrasting with less than 3% (129 out of a total of 4,859 looms) in Coventry.[173] Full details of the distribution of looms in 1838, derived from information contained in the *Fletcher Report*, are given in Figure 46.

---

173 Fletcher, p. 12.

AREA	Single Hand Loom			Plain Engine Loom			Jacquard Loom			TOTAL		Proportion of Looms		
	No.	% of this type of loom	% of all looms	No.	% of this type of loom	% of all looms	No.	% of this type of loom	% of all looms	No.	% of all looms	Single Hand-Loom	Plain Engine-Loom	Jacquard Loom
Coventry and Immediate Suburbs	129	1.72	0.98	3,452	98.57	26.11	1,278	57.36	9.67	4,859	36.76	2.65	71.04	26.30
Foleshill & Exhall	2,250	30.04	17.02	50	1.43	0.38	400	17.95	3.03	2,700	20.43	83.33	1.85	14.81
Ansty	10	0.13	0.08		0.00	0.00		0.00	0.00	10	0.08	100.00	0.00	0.00
Shilton	50	0.67	0.38		0.00	0.00		0.00	0.00	50	0.38	100.00	0.00	0.00
Sowe	250	3.34	1.89		0.00	0.00	30	1.35	0.23	280	2.12	89.29	0.00	10.71
Bedworth	1,000	13.35	7.56		0.00	0.00	320	14.36	2.42	1,320	9.99	75.76	0.00	24.24
Bulkington	800	10.68	6.05		0.00	0.00		0.00	0.00	800	6.05	100.00	0.00	0.00
Nuneaton & District	**3,000**	**40.06**	**22.69**		**0.00**	**0.00**	**200**	**8.98**	**1.51**	**3,200**	**24.21**	**93.75**	**0.00**	**6.25**
Total	7,489	100.00	56.65	3,502	100.00	26.49	2,228	100.00	16.85	1,3219	100.00	56.65	26.49	16.85

Fig. 46. Distribution of looms, by type, in Coventry and Warwickshire, 1838. Source: *Assistant Hand-Loom Weavers' Commissioners' Report Part IV* (*The Fletcher Report*) 1840.

Fletcher recorded that the population of Nuneaton had grown from 4,769 in 1801 to 7,799 in 1831, a very significant increase of almost 64% in just three decades. Unfortunately for those who had settled in the town in that period, the year 1831 also saw perhaps the worst economic depression ever to have hit the town, with more than 80% of the 4,219 looms in the Nuneaton area (denoted as including Chilvers Coton and Hartshill) being unemployed. This level was almost twice as high as that in Coventry, which included Radford and Stoke, and well above the average for all of the ribbon weaving locations in the area (65%) – see Figure 47.

Fletcher commented on the increasing use of more efficient and productive looms in the Midlands, where '*the single hand-loom was extensively superseded by the engine-loom, because of the new economy imposed by the Jacquard machinery... which in the single hand-loom could give the pattern only to a single breadth, but being equally available in the engine-loom for all the breadths that it may contain simultaneously.*' In his account of the undertaking system, i.e. manufacturing through the agency of local 'undertakers', or master weavers, Fletcher confirmed that the overwhelming majority of this trade took place only in the rural parishes to the north of Coventry, including Nuneaton. He further added that

Fig. 47. The scale of unemployed/redundant looms in Coventry and Warwickshire in 1831. Source: *Assistant Hand-Loom Weavers' Commissioners' Report Part IV (The Fletcher Report)* 1840.

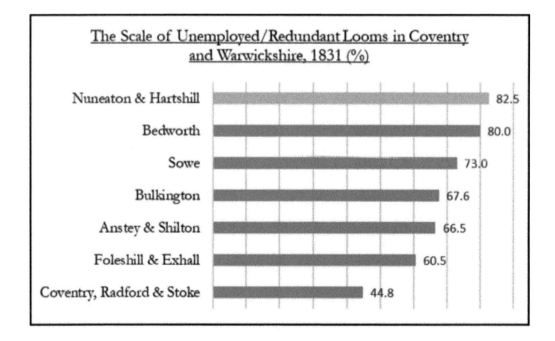

The Scale of Unemployed/Redundant Looms in Coventry and Warwickshire, 1831 (%)

Nuneaton & Hartshill — 82.5
Bedworth — 80.0
Sowe — 73.0
Bulkington — 67.6
Anstey & Shilton — 66.5
Foleshill & Exhall — 60.5
Coventry, Radford & Stoke — 44.8

Nuneaton's continued reliance on single hand-looms severely limited productivity and had been a critical factor behind the inexorable decline in silk ribbon weaving in the town and the increasing destitution in the population.

MORAL CONDITION

Fletcher's observations on the *'moral habits of the weavers and the moral constitution of the local community'* acknowledged the relationship between the moral circumstances existing in the locality and the amount earned by weavers for their work. He lamented only being able to undertake hasty inquiries due to limitations of time, resources and abilities, and presented therefore only *'hastily thrown together memoranda'*. They still make for fascinating reading though, and perhaps provide us with one of the most vivid and accurate accounts of what life would have been like for many people living in Nuneaton in the early 1830s.

He starts by referencing the conditions in Coventry and the weaving districts to its north in the 1790s. *'The mass of the labouring population… undisturbed by schools or by sectarianism, remained in a state of barbarism, as gross as it was consistent with the perpetuation of the race; the men without intelligence and without religion, working badly at irregular hours, and sotting in dirt and disorder nearly the rest of their time, including the whole of Sunday.'*[174]

Fletcher at first found it hard to credit the evidence of witnesses about the *'moral debasement'* of the area. He then quotes evidence from Richard Holmes, an undertaker (master weaver) from Foleshill: *'The mass of people… are brutally ignorant. It is not the population which has gone down into ignorance; it has never emerged from it. There is more profanity, more Sabbath-breaking, and more immorality than former. Their language is awfully depraved. Bastardy is greater than ever… at any little holiday time, the public-houses will be thronged with girls ready for the lowest excesses. Both sexes are great drinkers, chiefly of ale.'*[175]

---

174 Fletcher, p. 71.
175 Ibid., p. 76.

Another witness from Foleshill, Robert Cantrill, thought that the 'aggravated' situation that existed at that time was unprecedented and was causally linked to the persistent economic depression: '*A part, certainly, of the general misconduct is brought on by distress. Thinks it makes a man hopeless; and, when hopeless, he becomes desperate, and preys upon society; and then comes the last wretchedness* [extensive and aggravated thieving].'[176]

John Slingsby, an undertaker from Bulkington, described the habits of its people in depressing terms: '*The habits of the men altogether are shackling and profligate. The journeymen have commonly not a farthing's worth of anything on or off their persons which they could pawn or they would not long possess it. Many of the houses have no furniture but a stool and a table with perhaps an old chair; a loom, on which the man worked; and often neither bed nor bedstead. The girls, before marriage, are sometimes forced to find money for the debauches of their sweethearts. Certainly, seventeen out of every twenty are 'far gone' in the family way at marriage. They are altogether excessively rude and uncultivated.*'[177]

These descriptions of single hand-loom weaving communities in Foleshill and Bulkington were said to still apply largely to nearby Nuneaton. The Rev. King, the curate of St Nicolas Parish Church, was convinced that '*the poverty of the people prevents their attending public worship; and moral and religious instruction can therefore reach them only through the visits of clergymen, an influence which is necessarily limited.*'

The relieving officer of the Nuneaton Poor Law Union, Mr Ralphs, confirmed that '*the undertakers are for the most part very poor, and they are made poorer by the frequent change of patterns* [for ribbons], *which is now customary. Nuneaton and* [Chilvers] *Coton had always had an excess of parish business in the way of bastardy* [that arose] *from the habits of the weaving population, especially those of a Friday night. In many cases the young woman was enceinte* [pregnant] *before marriage.*'[178]

Fletcher lamented the lack of resident clergymen in the four chief parishes of the dispersed single-hand trade, i.e. Foleshill,

---

176 Fletcher, p. 76.
177 Ibid., p. 77.
178 Ibid., p. 78.

Bulkington, Nuneaton and Exhall, in '*districts that were so much demanding the services of moral and religious teachers*', with a stipendiary curate lacking the ability to '*master the evils which here surround him*'. The report was therefore suggesting that the absenteeism of the vicar of St Nicolas (R. Bruce Stopford) and the resultant lack of clerical capacity was causing '*moral and spiritual pollution almost as great as the physical*'. Stopford was vicar from 1803-1845 and was notorious for taking the income from the position and leaving an over-worked curate to look after the parish in his absence.[179] This dereliction of religious duty unfortunately occurred in the period of perhaps its greatest need in Nuneaton's history. The report contrasted this state of affairs with the success of Henry Bellairs, who had been the resident curate, then rector, of Bedworth since September 1819, who had successfully improved that town's conditions and reputation, aided by funds from the Nicholas Chamberlaine charities.[180]

Fletcher's analysis of the prevailing moral conditions included a link to increased criminality in the locality: '*For the single-hand trade of the country* (i.e. rural parishes) *not only exhibits the greatest demoralization at home, but helps to fill the criminal calendar of neighbouring counties.*' He concluded with the overall assessment that: '*the present generation of weavers have neither the moral habits, religious feelings, nor secular intelligence to retrieve them from the condition in which they exist.*'[181]

PHYSICAL CONDITION

Evidence gathered by Fletcher also related to the physical condition of the weavers, indicating a feebler constitution than that possessed by artisans generally in that they were '*persons of much inferior physical character, smaller of stature, of less muscular development and enjoying lower animal spirits*'. The report also noted that tuberculosis ('scrofula' – tubercular infection of the lymph nodes of the neck) was common among the weaving population,

---

179 Paterson & Rowney, pp. 22, 26.
180 Fletcher, p. 79.
181 Ibid., pp. 81–2.

and that cholera was not unknown.[182] Indeed, tuberculosis of the neck was the cause of death of James Horobin, husband of Polly Button's third child, Hannah, in 1862.

Fletcher then went on to consider the impact of such physical depression with the mental character of the weavers, '*Anxiety as to the circumstances of their families and their trade is very conspicuous, and insanity is most frequent among them. The anxiety is greatly aggravated by the fluctuating nature of the trade*'.[183]

The work itself resulted in significant ill-health effects, arising from '*the resting of the breast against the loom, the constrained position, the want of air, and the frequent over-exhaustion*'. The physical inferiority induced by the weaving appeared to Fletcher to be the main obstacle to workers moving to any other employment, so that a sense of entrapment in the trade may have resulted, with the population having a '*once weavers and always weavers*' mentality.[184]

Charles B Nankivell was the surgeon to Coventry's Self-Supporting Dispensary that was instituted in the spring of 1831 and gained a membership of nearly 3,000 people in the remaining years of the decade. The scale of the health impact on the weavers of Coventry can be shown by the fact that about 70% of them received treatment in one year.[185] Fletcher quotes Nankivell's view that, '*There were instances of great poverty, in the cases especially of the few single-hand weavers in the city*',[186] again confirming the much greater deprivation amongst this class of weaver. Nuneaton had a much greater number and proportion of single hand-loom weavers and was therefore likely to have been even more adversely affected in this regard.

Thomas Henry Prosser, an ex-Bow Street Runner and head of the Police in Coventry, stated that: '*The houses of some of the weavers of the lower classes are in the most wretched state, with only a little straw and a coverlet for a bed; plenty of children, but scarcely a chair to sit down upon.*'[187]

---

182 Ibid., p. 300.
183 Ibid., p. 301.
184 Ibid., p. 301.
185 Hodgkinson, p. 246.
186 Fletcher, p. 301.
187 Ibid., p. 302.

GENERAL BOARD OF HEALTH REPORT (1849)

Our knowledge and understanding of the insanitary conditions that existed in Nuneaton in this period comes primarily from a major report by George Thomas Clark into the public health of the town, published in 1849. Although written 17 years after Polly Button's murder, it would appear that no effective action had been taken to address the underlying problems in the intervening years. The rapid commercial growth of the town and the need to quickly and cheaply house the rising workforce had resulted in the construction of over-crowded and squalid courts in ribbon development along Abbey Street. A clear indicator of the atrocious state of public health in Nuneaton at this time was the town's first ever outbreak of cholera that erupted in Abbey Street in 1832, the year of Polly Button's murder.

The first incidence of cholera in England had been reported in Sunderland in the autumn of October 1831, from where it had rapidly spread to other parts of the country. Awareness, if not anxieties, were heightened in many towns that had experienced rapid industrial, commercial and population growth as outbreaks of this devastating infectious disease began to occur more widely. This was demonstrated locally in an entry by Robert Evans (George Eliot's father) in his diary for 15 April 1832 which reads: *'Went to Coton Church. I was taken with a Bowel complaint today and had a bad night I thought the Collers [cholera] had leazed me.'*[188] The first recorded case of a burial due to a death from cholera in Nuneaton was that of Thomas Moore, aged 50, of Wheat Lane on 8 September 1832. The next few weeks saw the disease spread through the town, with entries in the *Nuneaton Diary* recording that, *'Cholera broke out in a yard at the middle of Abbey Street, several proved fatal'* (October) and *'The cholera is still raging but more so in the Abbey St., many deaths have occurred'* (November). The insanitary courts of Abbey Street provided perfect conditions for cholera to spread. Indeed, in the first few months of the outbreak the register of burials at St Nicolas Parish Church recorded that more than half of the deaths due to cholera were of people living

'The cholera is still raging... many deaths have occurred.'

---

188 Evans.

in Abbey Street (51.7%), followed by Bond End (16%) and Back Lane (10.7%), reflecting the likely degree of deprivation present in these areas. This was not unusual, with one source asserting that, *'In Great Britain, as elsewhere, cholera fixed its residence among the most needy and squalid classes of the community.'*[189] Fortunately, it seems that the disease gradually disappeared in the course of the autumn and winter that followed.

Sir Edwin Chadwick was a pioneer in public health and his work on the control of cholera, detailed in his *Report on an Inquiry into the Sanitary Conditions of the Labouring Population of Great Britain* published in 1842, resulted in the Public Health Act of 1848. It was under the 1848 Act that George Thomas Clark was commissioned by the General Board of Health to undertake an investigation and report into the sewerage, drainage, supply of water and the sanitary conditions of the parishes of Nuneaton and Chilvers Coton.

George Thomas Clark (1809–1898) was a man of wide interests, many skills and tremendous energy. He served as an engineer under Isambard Kingdom Brunel on the construction of the Great Western Railway and the Taff Vale Railway and, in the 1840s, worked in India on a variety of engineering projects. On his return to England he came to the notice of the General Board of Health for an article on sanitary reform in *The Westminster Review* and was appointed as a superintending inspector. Between 1849 and 1851, Clark produced sixty-three reports on the sanitary condition of forty-six towns and villages, including one covering Nuneaton and Chilvers Coton.

Clark's week-long visit to Nuneaton began on 27 December 1848 and included public sittings to gather evidence in the Town Hall, then located in Market Place. Noting that the town was *'long and straggling'*, he identified three roads containing the main areas of habitation which included Abbey Street (where Polly Button lived) which was *'clustered with houses for three quarters of a mile'*. The mortality rate in the town in 1841 had been 30.7 per 1,000, well above the threshold to trigger concerns, although this had declined somewhat but to a still worryingly high rate of 26.7 per 1,000 by 1848.[190] It is not known what

---

189 Burke & Dodsley, p. 306.
190 Clark, para. 16.

the mortality rate in Nuneaton had been in 1832, as this had been prior to the collection and use of public health statistics. However, given that cholera had made such a profound impact on the town's population, it is likely to have been in excess of 30 per 1,000. Such a level has been deemed to be 'highly destructive to human life' and confirms the existence of appalling sanitary conditions.

In considering the conditions in the town during his visit, Clark found ample cause for the unusually high death rate. His attention was directed to certain localities, chiefly courts, which probably would have included those in Upper Abbey Street where Polly Button had lived only 17 years previously. He identified these as '*the seats of fever and smallpox... which were ill-paved, damp, undrained, and in a very filthy and offensive condition*' – a description Clark

Fig. 48. Part of a typical court and entry in Abbey Street, Nuneaton.

suggested that could be applied '*in some considerable degree to nearly the whole of Nuneaton. I find part of the Abbey Street and Back Lane to be very sickly quarters. In these places the greater part of the population are lodged in courts communicating with the street by a narrow covered entry, and open to the fields behind it. They consist of from 5 to 15 houses each, with one or two privies in common, a large open tank or cesspool; a pump is generally very near the cesspool, often a pigstye. Usually towards the field is an open stagnant ditch. In many of these courts is a common soughing tile-drain, intended to take the surface water, but fitted up with a large grating and catch-pit from whence bad smells ascend.*'[191] Figure 48 shows a typical court of the area, with the door in the entry leading to Abbey Street.

---

191 Clark, paras 18–19.

Clark naturally focused his concerns on foul drainage:

> *The cesspool is the greatest evil and the most constantly present. It is often 10 to 12 feet square and very deep. Into it are discharged the contents of the privy, and all the rubbish and filth of every kind from the houses. It is emptied only once or twice annually, and is in consequence often heaped up far above the top of its side walls, so as to expose a greatly increased offensive surface. In some cases the cesspool is above the highway, and the contents percolate through the walls or flow along the gutters into the street. In one other instance its walls were those of a dwelling-house, and the soil oozed through upon the floor, rendering the house from time to time uninhabitable. In one case the cesspool was enclosed by a dwelling-house in which were persons living on each side of and above it. To these cesspools and piggeries are sometimes added slaughter-houses, stables, depots for dung collected in the streets, and various other nuisances.*[192]

Clark recorded the sources of nuisance and potential disease as comprising 287 pigsties, 385 privies, 346 cesspools and 15 slaughterhouses. The report also pointed out the inadequacy of the piped sewerage system, with only irregularly laid and very short lengths installed in the town. Abbey Street only contained a total of 210 yards of surface water sewer which covered less than 20% of the street and '*even these drains are reported to be very badly laid as to level. The drainage into these from the courts and alleys is by an ordinary agricultural soughing tile-drain* [soughing or drainage tiles had a flat tile forming the floor of the drain and an arched tile placed on top]. *In other cases these soughs are carried into open stagnant ditches at the backs of the premises.*' The contents of the privies and cesspools were emptied once or twice annually when they were '*disturbed and carted off in broad daylight to the great annoyance of everybody*'. After being carted off, the contents of the cesspool were usually stored in a heap by the roadside. Clark also recorded that there was no individual house drainage, '*in most cases the slops of the house being emptied into the yard and in others into the main street from the door or window.*'[193]

---

192 Clark, paras 20–21.
193 Ibid., paras 27, 33, 38, 40.

There was no permanent piped water supply in Nuneaton. Inhabitants made use of wells (varying from 9 feet to 25 feet deep), from which water was obtained by one or two pumps in each court.[194] Given the seepage from cesspools described in Clark's report and the relatively shallow depth of some of the wells, it is perhaps not surprising at all that there had been an outbreak of cholera in the town in 1832.

Clark, whose experience in matters of public health was extensive given that he authored more than 60 reports on sanitary conditions in urban areas, made scathing comments about the condition of the 4¾ miles of streets and highways in the town, saying that he had '*seldom seen public ways in a worse condition*'.[195]

In summarising his findings, Clark confirmed that the '*public nuisances consist of open dung-heaps, stagnant and foul pools and ditches, unmade or ill-made roads, privies having no drain and exposed to highways*'.[196] '*The present state of the town I found the subject of universal complaint. The darkness* [arising from a dispute between rural government and the parish that had led to gas lighting being discontinued] *adds materially to the labours of the police and promotes various gross immoralities. These, the darkness itself and the dirty condition of the public ways combine to render Nuneaton a place through which a respectable female could not safely walk after nightfall.*'[197]

---

194 Ibid., para. 41.
195 Ibid., para. 45.
196 Ibid., para. 58.
197 Ibid., para. 51.

ANNEXE 3: A TRANSCRIPT

OF THE FIRST NEWSPAPER REPORT –
COVENTRY HERALD, 24 FEBRUARY 1832

[Note: Text, including spelling, is as printed in the original article.]

During the past week, an extraordinary sensation prevailed in the town of Nuneaton, owing to the perpetration of an appalling murder, which took place on Saturday evening last, in that neighbourhood, on the body of an unfortunate woman, named Mary Green, otherwise better known by the name of Polly Button. The following are the circumstances connected with the horrible transaction: a similar one has not occurred in that neighbourhood within the recollection of the oldest inhabitant:

The wretched woman Green, who in no small degree was the victim of her own gross immorality, was a native of Nuneaton, a single woman and lived in a small house at the top of Abbey-street, together with five of her own illegitimate children, the fruit of an almost indiscriminate intercourse. For the last three years she had been co-habiting with a man named John Danks, by whom she had one child in the year 1829, and against whom she had affiliated another three weeks since, and of which she was eight months advanced in pregnancy. Owing to this connection with Danks, who was a married man, various quarrels ensued between Danks, his wife, and Green, and a consequent known dislike existed between the parties.

On the evening of Saturday last, as it is reported, Danks went to the house of Green, and having called her out, they proceeded across a field at the rear of the wretched woman's dwelling in the direction of a hovel, belonging to Mr Astley; of this particular notice was not taken by the person who saw them, owing to their having been seen to go towards the same place on former occasions. Bed-time, however, arrived, and Green not returning home, a search was made for her in the neighbourhood by her daughter, but nothing was heard of her until the following morning, about eight o'clock, when the body was found in a field within twenty yards of the above-mentioned hovel, weltering in blood, the head being nearly severed from the body, and other marks of brutality upon her.

The alarm having been given, suspicion immediately fell upon Danks. Mr Haddin, constable, went to his house, but not finding him at home, he went towards Nuneaton Common, to which place he had been informed Danks had gone. Having arrived on the Common, he met Danks, took him into custody, and conveyed him to the Red Lion public house.

Here Danks was informed by Mr Haddin that the body of Green was found, and that he arrested him on suspicion of having committed the murder, to which the prisoner with much indifference replied, "Well, if she is murdered, I know nothing of it." His clothes were then searched, and having presented a suspicious appearance, they were taken from him and replaced by others, after which he was taken to the Guard House, in Nuneaton.

By this time a great concourse had assembled round the prison. On going up the steps the prisoner took off his hat and waved it three or four times above his head. Danks's wife was next taken into custody, and confined in Mr Haddin's house. The body of Green was removed to her miserable abode, and a number of respectable gentlemen of the town were engaged during the day in endeavouring to obtain information connected with the affair.

On Monday morning, Messrs. Burton, Buchanan, and the Rev Mr Docker and Mr Haddin went to the house of Danks, and on examining the premises, an apron, stained apparently with blood, was found in a pot of water, of which there was a quantity of potash; this, together with other circumstances, led to the opinion that Danks's wife was also concerned in the murder, and in the evening the above gentlemen went to her, when she vehemently disclaimed all participation in the murder, but acknowledged that on Sunday morning, when in bed with her husband, he said to her, "Well, Polly Button will never disturb another family, for I cut her head almost off, and threw the knife into the hedge." This admission led to an important discovery; the field adjoining the one in which the murder was committed was searched next morning, and on the other side of the hedge, as stated by Danks's wife, a pocket knife, covered with blood was found, which, it is said, has been identified as belonging to Danks.

On Tuesday morning, at ten o'clock, an inquest was held at The Britannia public house, before W. H. Seymour, Gent., Coroner, and the following respectable jury:

Mr William Burton. Foreman
Mr William Ball
Mr William Swinnerton
Mr Thomas Swinnerton
Mr Robert Arnold
Mr John Tabernor
Mr Isaac Swinnerton
Mr Thomas Robinson
Mr George Taylor
Mr Richard Clay
Mr Richard Wood
Mr Thomas Ball

The examination of witnesses continued until four o'clock, when an adjournment took place to the following morning.

On Wednesday morning the investigation was resumed and closed at twelve o'clock. The prisoner Danks was then brought into the room ironed, and placed before the Coroner, for the purpose of having the evidence read over to him. He is a man about five feet four inches in height, between 40 and 50 years of age, by trade a carpenter, and by no means of a forbidding countenance, nor was there anything in his appearance indicative of a mind capable of committing the crime with which he stood charged. He listened with particular attention to the evidence, and although an illiterate man, displayed much tact in interrogating some of the witnesses.

He neither denied or acknowledged the offence; and throughout the whole, maintained a more than ordinary degree of nerve and self-

possession. At his request, two persons were sent for as witnesses for him, and during the absence of the messenger, he was asked by Mr Haddin, if he wished any refreshments, to which he replied that he should like a little bread and cheese; with this and a glass of ale he was supplied. He ate with avidity, and on taking up the ale glass, he drank the healths of the persons present.

The persons whom he sent for being examined, the room was ordered to be cleared, and the Jury, after a short consultation, returned the following verdict–

"That the deceased, Mary Green, was wilfully murdered, and that John Danks is the person who murdered her."

The prisoner was now taken to the Guard House, followed by an immense crowd and in going along was assailed with groans and hisses. There being no evidence against his wife, she was ordered to be set at liberty; previous to which she seemed as if in a state of derangement, sometimes crying, and at others rolling her eyes about with a wild and vacant stare at those around her.

On the morning of the day on which she was liberated, being confined in Mr Haddin's house, she availed herself of a temporary absence of the person who had her in charge, walked down stairs, passed out of the house unnoticed, and ran furiously up the street, until she came to a house the door of which was open. The owner of the house not being in the house, she entered and fastened the door; which being forced open, the miserable being was found sitting in one corner of a room upstairs, in the utmost terror.

The deceased was about 40 years of age, of low stature, and of disagreeable appearance.

The above are the principal circumstances connected with the affair.

Yesterday, Danks passed through Coventry in a cart, on his way to Warwick, where he will be tried at the next assizes. Since writing the above, we are informed that Danks has made a full confession of his guilt.

ANNEXE 4:

TRANSCRIPT OF THE EXECUTION BROADSIDE –

'LIFE, TRIAL AND EXECUTION OF JOHN DANKS'

[Note: Spellings are as printed in the original document and are indicative of a 'rush job' to catch the market for selling the broadside to the attendant crowd.]

Life, Trial and Execution of John Danks, aged 45, for the Wilful murder of Mary Green, at Nuneaton, who suffered this morning (Monday) April the 2nd, at Warwick

> *The following are the particulars connceted with the horrid transaction: – The wretched woman Green, who, in no small degree, was the victim of her own gross immorality, was a native of Nuneaton, a single woman and lived in a small house, at the top of Abbey-street together with her five illigitimate children, the fruit of an almost indiscriminate intercourse. For the last three years she had been cohabi wit the man Danks, by whom she had one child in the year 1829, and against whom, she had sworn another, three weeks since, and of which she was advanced eight months. Owing to this connexion with Danks, who was a married man various quarrels ensued between Danks his wife and Green, On the Saturday, Danks went to the house of Green and called her out, they proceeded across a field, in the rear of the woman's dwelling, and in the direction of a hovel. Bed arrived and Green not returned home, search was made, but nothing was heard until the following morning when the body was found in a field about twenty yards from the hovel, weltering in*

blood, and her head nearly severed from her body. The alarm having been given. suspicion fell on Danks, Mr Haddin, constable, went to Nuneaton Common, and took Danks into custody, and conveyed him to Red Lion pnblic house. Here Danks was informed, that the body of Green was found, and that he arrested him on the charge of murder, to which the prisoner replied, "Well if she is murdered I know nothing of it". Dank's wife was then taken into custody, and on examining the premises, and apron stained with blood, was found in a pot of water, this together with other circumstances led to the opinion that Dank's wife was concerned in the murder, and in the morning of Sunday she acknowledged when in bed with her husband he said to her, "Well, Mary Green will disturb no more families for I cut the head almost off, and threw the knife into the hedge." This admission led to and important discovery, for the field was searched, next morning and the knife found which was identified as belonging to Danks.

On Friday morning last the unfortunate man placed at the bar, and when the above were clearly proved by evidence, and a trial which lasted upwards of six hours, the Jury returned of Guilty. Mr Bayley* proceeded to pass the awful sentence of the law, in a most impressive manner, and begg'd of the prisoner duriug the few hours he had to live that he would employ them in seeking mercy from that God in whom mercy would be found.

EXECUTION

Since condemnation, Danks has assiduous in his preparation to meet his awful fate, on Sunday morning after receiving the Sacrament, he confessed that he alone it was that committed the murder, acknowledged the justness of his sentence, in the afternoon he took leave of his wife and children**, which was truly affecting. He then gave himself to prayer and passed a good night, at seven o'clock this morning the chaplain was in attendance administered the consolation of religion, when every preparation was made, the prison bell*** began to toll, and the slow processioa moved to the platform, and minister prayed for a short time, when the fatal bolt was and he ceased to live. A vastcrowd of people were collected to witness.
Blomly Prietor Coventry

Notes of correction and clarification:

* * The presiding Judge was not Baron Bayley but Justice James Parke.
* ** He had no children with Jane, his second wife. The children attending would have been Ann (aged 26) and John (aged 23) from his first marriage.
* *** The bell that tolled was not the prison bell but that of the nearby St Mary's Church.

ACKNOWLEDGEMENTS

Uncovering the full story behind the murder of Polly Button was to have been a project for my retirement. However, having prematurely dipped my toe in the water to see what information might be available online I was hooked and just got stuck in to the research. As I uncovered more and more details about the life, times and murder of Polly Button it became apparent that her story comprised several important, distinct and fascinating elements. I hope I have done justice to the telling of that story. I would not have been able to do so without the involvement and support of a wide range of people, including family, friends, local historians, archivists and other researchers. It has been extremely rewarding to have been the beneficiary of such interest, expertise, support and, indeed, friendship. There are a number of people that warrant specific acknowledgement for their involvement.

I'm grateful for the unwavering help, advice and encouragement throughout the project from my partner in life as well as in (this) crime, Tina. As a direct descendant of Polly Button, she was the catalyst for my interest. I must also acknowledge the support from my two children, Tayo and Rheanna-Fay, whose patience throughout and expertise when needed was much appreciated.

I received significant and valued support from a number of local historians, namely David Paterson, John Burton and Peter Lee. Their support, guidance and feedback throughout has been invaluable.

Teresa Evans worked with her father, Cyril Marden, to research and write the first book about Polly Button's murder in 1977. Once I'd established the initial contact with Teresa, subsequent discussions about our experiences of researching Polly Button's story proved both informative and enjoyable. She also unearthed a unique photograph of the Polly Button stone as it was when her father had found it amongst a store of reclaimed building materials in the yard of the Nuneaton Borough Council's depot. I am also grateful to Nigel Pratt for permission to reproduce a number of his original illustrations in Cyril Marden's book.

Stuart Gill of SCG Cartography and Design worked wonders in producing new maps, comprising a georeferenced version of the original map produced for the trial of the murderer, John Danks, and a map that overlaid these details onto the present-day street layout.

Thanks also to Richie Cumberlidge at More Visual Limited whose considerable experience and talents in graphic design and book covers are self-evident in both the cover for this book and several illustrations within it.

The incredibly talented illustrator, David Lupton, brought to life the image I had nurtured in my mind of Polly Button lying dead in front of her distressed, wretched and ragged children. A door had been used to carry her body the 250 metres or so from the scene of the murder back to her dismal abode. The darkness of such an image, derived from one I had first seen in a cycle of illustrations called *A Weavers' Revolt*, by the German artist Kathe Kollwitz, has been perfectly realised by David.

Pat Thomas, one of America's leading medical illustrators, has provided the first ever visual representation of the wounds to Polly Button's throat based on information gleaned from two original source descriptions. The quality of her work is clear for all to see. For expertise on matters medical contained within the book I am grateful to Dr Stephen Heap (a descendant of John Danks) and Elisha Whelan for their advice.

I am indebted to Alison James, who joined the project as it's official photographer and brought her considerable skills to bear in producing some great photographs for this book, the project's two related Facebook groups and other social media.

Specific credit also needs to be given to Professor Fred Burwick, Research Professor at the University of California, Los Angeles, whose research for his major work *British Drama of the Industrial*

Revolution led to the discovery of the existence of the first play written about the murder of Polly Button, performed within two years of her death. The play, *The Ghost Walk of Weddington*, was found in an archive in Greenwich, which was subsequently transferred in its entirety to the University of Bristol's Theatre Collection. Jill Sullivan, archivist at the University of Bristol, has tried, so far in vain, to locate the manuscript of the play which appears to have been mis-filed at some stage before the transfer. I continue to hope that the play will eventually resurface and be made available for further research.

Karen Youles and Helen Carpenter have generously contributed ideas and advice for how best to get the incredible story of Polly Button to as wide an audience as possible. Their role in advising on the marketing and communications for the project has been central to its success. Adam Gajic designed and created the impressive website to support the project and facilitate online purchasing of the book (www.pollybutton.com).

Site visits were made to a number of locations as part of my research. One of the most interesting was the tour and explanation of the workings of the Crown Court at Warwick given by Colin Jones (WCC Estates Manager). Ann O'Brien (Facilities Manager at Legal & General's Head Office) facilitated a visit to photograph the portrait of Serjeant John Adams, a prosecuting counsel at the trial of John Danks. David F Wills (Squire Law Librarian, Cambridge University Library) organised a visit by Tayo Moore to photograph the portrait of Andrew Amos, the other prosecuting counsel at Danks's trial. Louise Essex and Gill Robinson of the Local Studies team at Nuneaton Library, gave freely of their time, arranging for me to photograph relevant parts of the *Nuneaton Diary* and other materials held by the library, and organising illustrated talks about Polly Button in advance of publication. All such visits provided some welcome and enjoyable variation in my research.

Archivists who responded helpfully to my requests for assistance included David Hodgkinson (Warwickshire County Record Office), staff at the Walsall Local History Centre, Clare Starkie (Museums Sheffield) and Joan Self (National Meteorological Archive).

Angela Hall, an Advanced Professional Member of the Society of Indexers, compiled the index for the book, an important element that I'm confident readers will find both comprehensive and useful given the nature and extent of the background to Polly Button's story.

Helpful feedback on early drafts of the text was given by family, friends and colleagues. Particular thanks go to David Paterson, John Burton, Peter Lee, Chris Richards, Teresa Evans, John Walton, Lindsey Millington, Brenda Evans, Sue Foster and John Veasey.

The Polly Button Project has been well supported throughout by two Facebook groups with an interest in the history of Nuneaton: Nuneaton Memories (https://www.facebook.com/groups/NuneatonMemories/) and Nuneaton & Bedworth Local and Family History – Notes & Queries (https://www.facebook.com/groups/nuneatonhistory). I'm grateful to their founders/administrators (Mark Palmer and Peter Lee, respectively) for their support in helping to promote Polly Button's story.

The final phase of the project was to translate five years of research and writing into the production of a book that people would be attracted to and enjoy reading (putting the dreadful events at the heart of the story to one side, of course). I will be forever grateful to the team at Matador (Joe Shillito, Alexa Davies and Lauren Bailey in particular) for their excellent and efficient work in producing and marketing the book that I envisioned.

This account of the story of Polly Button would not have been possible without the collective interest, support and endeavour of all those named above – and I thank them all.

All author profits from the sale of this book will be used to benefit three local charities and good causes: a Nuneaton women's refuge run by a leading UK domestic violence charity, Chilvers Coton Centre Trust (Heritage Centre) and Nuneaton Memories.

BIBLIOGRAPHY/REFERENCES

Acton, W. (1857). *Prostitution – considered in its moral, social and sanitary aspects in London and other large cities with proposals for the control and prevention of its abundant evils*. London: John Churchill & Sons.

Amos, A. (1832). On the Possibility of Voluntary Locomotion After the Complete Division of the Carotid Artery and Other Large Vessels of the Throat (from a lecture on Medical Jurisprudence by Professor Amos at the London University). *London Medical Gazette*. Vol. X.

Anon. (1833). *The Ghost Walk of Weddington*. Warwickshire: Manuscript. (University of Bristol Theatre Collection).

Archenholtz, I. (1788). *The British Mercury, or Annals of History, Politics, Manners, Literature, Arts etc of the British Empire, Vol IV, Issues 1–13*. Hamburg: Hoffman.

Astley, J. (1810–1845). *The Nuneaton Diary: Memorandum Book of Occurrences at Nuneaton (Volume 1: January 1810 to April 1825/ Volume 2: May 1825 to 27 Nov 1845)*. Nuneaton: Manuscript held at Nuneaton Library.

Barfoot, P. & Wilkes, J. (1791–98). *Universal British Directory of Trade, Commerce and Manufacture – Volume the Fifth*. London: Universal British Directory.

Beck, T. R. & Beck J. B. (1863). *Elements of Medical Jurisprudence. Vol. 2*. 12th ed. Philadelphia: J.B. Lippencott & Co.

Blomly. (1832). *The Life, Trial and Execution of John Danks*. Execution Broadside in Historical & Special Collections, Harvard Law School Library.

Burke, E. & Dodsley, J. (1833). *The Annual Register, or a View of the History, Politics and Literature of the Year 1832*. London: J. Dodsley.

Brookes, J. *Weddington Castle*. Available: http://www.weddingtoncastle. co.uk/1800-ndash-1900ad.html. Accessed 9 September 2017.

Burwick, F. (2015). *British Drama of the Industrial Revolution.* Cambridge: Cambridge University Press.

Bush, S. (2009). *The Silk Industry.* 2nd ed. Botley: Shire Publications Ltd.

Clark, G. (March 1849). *Report to the General Board of Health on a Preliminary Enquiry into the Sewerage, Drainage, and Supply of Water, and the Sanitary Condition of the Inhabitants of the Parishes of Nuneaton and Chilvers Coton.* London: HMSO.

Clarke, R. (2017). *The Process of Judicial Hanging.* Available: http://www. capitalpunishmentuk.org/hanging2.html. Accessed 27 July 2017.

Clayton, D. (2018). *Decisive Victory – The Battle of the Sambre, 4 November 1918.* Warwick: Helion & Company Ltd.

Committee on Ribbon Weavers (March 1818). *First Report of Minutes of Evidence taken before the committee appointed to consider of the several petitions relating to ribbon weavers.* London: House of Commons.

Committee on Ribbon Weavers (April/May 1818). *Second Report of Minutes of evidence taken before the committee appointed to consider of the several petitions relating to ribbon weavers.* London: House of Commons.

Davenport, R. (2015). The first stages of the mortality transition in England: a perspective from evolutionary biology. Available: https://www.geog. cam.ac.uk/research/projects/migrationmortalitymedicalisation/ pdf2.pdf. Last accessed 7 July 2018.

Evans, R. (1830). *Diary entry for 15 April 1832.* Available: https:// robertevans1830.wordpress.com/author/nuneatonmuseum/ page/17/. Last accessed 25 July 2017.

Fairey, Charles E. (2018). *Protective Devices, Apotropaic Symbols and Witch Marks; on Historic Buildings; with examples from Cheshire, Shropshire and Staffordshire.* Available: https://sites.google.com/site/ charlesfaireyhistorian/publications/protective-devices-apotropaic- symbols-and-witch-marks. Last accessed 20 August 2018.

Flanders, J. (2012). *The Victorian City – Everyday Life in Dickens' London.* London: Atlantic Books. [Chapter 15 – The Red-Lit Streets to Death]

Fletcher, J. (1840). *Reports from Assistant Hand-Loom Weavers' Commissioners, Part IV. Report by Joseph Fletcher, Secretary to the Commission, on the Midland Districts of England.* London: Her Majesty's Stationery Office.

Gavin, H. (1848). *Sanitary Ramblings: Being Sketches and Illustrations of Bethnal Green.* London: Churchill.

GB Historical GIS/University of Portsmouth, *Nuneaton and Bedworth District through time | Population Statistics | Total Population, A Vision of Britain through Time.* URL: http://www.visionofbritain.org.uk/ unit/10105328/cube/TOT_POP. Accessed: 28 July 2017.

General Register Office (1852). *Eleventh Annual Report of the Registrar-General of Births, Deaths, and Marriages in England.* London: Her Majesty's Stationery Office.

Green, D. (1985). A Map for Mayhew's London: The Geography of Poverty in the Mid-Nineteenth Century. *London Journal.* 11 (2), pp. 115–126.

Hodgkinson, R. (1967). *The Origins of the National Health Service: The Medical Services of the New Poor Law, 1834–1871.* Berkeley: University of California Press.

Hollingshead, J. (1861). *Ragged London in 1861.* London: Smith, Elder & Co.

Humphreys, Noel A. (Ed.) (1885). *Vital Statistics – A Memorial Volume of Selections from The Reports and Writings of William Farr.* London: The Sanitary Institute.

Hussey, A. & Inman, D. (1921). The Fifth Division in the Great War. London: Nisbet & Co.

Jebbett, A. (1974). Old Nuneaton. Imprint: Nuneaton Library.

Jones, G. (2004). *James Parke, Baron Wensleydale (1782–1868).* Available: http://www.oxforddnb.com/view/article/21283. Last accessed 19 May 2015.

Levin, A. (2008). *Prostitution in Nineteenth-century England.* Available: https://ubcatlas.files.wordpress.com/2012/04/2008-levin.pdf. Accessed 10 March 2018.

Logan, W. (1843). *An exposure, from personal observation, of female prostitution in London, Leeds and Rochdale, and especially the city of Glasgow, with remarks on the cause, extent, results and remedy of the evil.* 2nd ed. Glasgow: Gallie & Fleckfield.

Long, G. (Ed.) (1843). *The Penny Cyclopaedia of the Society for the Diffusion of Useful Knowledge. Vol. XXVII Wales – Zygophyllaceae.* London: Charles Knight & Co.

London Gazette (1832). *Bulletins of State Intelligence, etc. 1832.* London: London Gazette.

Marden, C. (1977). *The Murder of Polly Button.* Nuneaton: Nuneaton Library. (Typescript photocopy).

Mayhew, H. (1861). *London Labour and the London Poor – Volume 4: Cyclopedia of the Condition and Earnings Those Who Will Not Work.* London: Charles Griffin & Company.

Merrick, G. (1890). *Work Among the Fallen – As Seen in the Prison Cells.* London: Ward, Lock.

Moss, J. (2011). *In and Around Haunted Nuneaton (Ill-Fated Polly Button).* Available: http://www.weddingtoncastle.co.uk/

uploads/1/9/5/1/19515001/ill_fated_polly_button.pdf. Last accessed 9 February 2019.

Muscutt, R. (2011). *The Life, Trial and Hanging of Mary Ball*. Dereham: Broadlands Books Ltd.

Paterson, D. & Rowney, I. (2007). *A short history of the parish church of Saint Nicolas, Nuneaton*. 2nd ed. Nuneaton: Self-published.

Pennant, T. (1811) *The Journey from Chester to London*. London: Printed for Wilkie and Robinson & Others.

Pigot, J. (1828). *Pigot and Co.'s National Commercial Directory for 1828-9*. London: J. Pigot & Co.

Pigot, J. (1835). *Pigot and Co.'s National Commercial Directory for 1835*. London: J. Pigot & Co.

Rickman, R. (1831). *Comparative Account of the Population of Great Britain in the Years 1801, 1811, 1821, and 1831; with the Annual Value of Real Property in the Year 1815: Also, a Statement of Progress in the Inquiry Regarding the Occupations of Families and Persons, and the Duration of Life, as Required by the Population Act of 1830*. London: General Register Office.

Royden, A. (1916). *Downward Paths – An inquiry into the causes which contribute to the making of the prostitute*. London: G. Bell & Sons Ltd.

Searby, P. (1972). *Weavers and freemen in Coventry, 1820–1861: social and political traditionalism in an early Victorian town*. PhD thesis. Coventry: University of Warwick.

Smith, B. (1991). Poor Polly Button. In: *Warwickshire Murders*. Newbury: Countryside Books.

Select Committee – Hand Loom Weavers (July 1835). *Report from the Select Committee on Hand Loom Weavers' Petitions (Minutes of Evidence)*. London: House of Commons.

Select Committee – Hand Loom Weavers (August 1835). *Analysis of Evidence taken before Select Committees on Hand-Loom Weavers' Petitions (1834–1835)*. London: House of Commons.

Select Committee on the Silk Trade (1832). *Report from the Select Committee on the Silk Trade*. London: House of Commons.

Tait, W. (1840). *Magdalenism – An enquiry into the extent, causes and consequences of prostitution in Edinburgh*. Edinburgh: Rickard.

Taylor, A. (1843). *Elements of Medical Jurisprudence, Interspersed with a Copious Selection of Curious and Instructive Cases and Analyses of Opinions Delivered at Coroners' Inquests*. London: Deacon.

Turton, K. (2010). A Deadly Secret. In: *Warwickshire Murders*. Stroud: The History Press (First published in 2007 by Sutton Publishing Ltd.)

Walford, W. (1857). *Hardwicke's Annual Biography for 1857 containing Original and Selected Memoirs of Celebrated Characters Who Have Died During the Year 1856*. London: Hardwicke.

Walkowitz, J. (1980). *Prostitution and Victorian Society – Women, Class and the State*. Cambridge: Cambridge University Press.

White, W. (1834). *History, Gazetteer, and Directory of Staffordshire*. Sheffield: Robert Leader.

Wilkinson, K. (Ed.) (1925). *The History of the Birmingham Medical School, 1825–1925*. Birmingham: Cornish Brothers.

Williams, R. (1999). A Social and Military History of the 1/8th Battalion, the Royal Warwickshire Regiment, in the Great War. Available: https://core.ac.uk/download/pdf/78049.pdf. Last accessed 8th February 2019.

Woods, R. & Woodward, J. (Eds.) (1984). Urban Disease and Mortality in Nineteenth Century England. London: Batsford.

West, W. (1830). *The History, Topography and Directory of Warwickshire*. Birmingham: Wrightson.

Veasey, E. (2002). *Nuneaton – A History*. Chichester: Phillimore & Co. Ltd.

LIST OF ILLUSTRATIONS

100	Fig. 29. The site of Danks's execution – outside Warwick gaol, Barrack Street, Warwick. Photograph © Steve Moore.
101	Fig. 30. The scaffold in front of Warwick Gaol. Original illustration in Cyril Marden's *The Murder of Polly Button*. Reproduced by kind permission of Nigel Pratt.
102	Fig. 31. Entry in the *Nuneaton Diary* for 13 April 1832 recording the execution of Danks. Courtesy of Nuneaton Library Local Studies Collection, Warwickshire County Council. Photograph © Steve Moore.
103	Fig. 32. Trials Broadside 331: '*Life, Trial and Execution of John Danks*'. Image courtesy of Historical & Special Collections, Harvard Law School Library.
105	Fig. 33. William Sands Cox. Lithograph by T. H. Maguire, 1854. Credit: Wellcome Library, London. Image courtesy of Wellcome Images, a website operated by Wellcome Trust, a global charitable foundation based in the United Kingdom. images@wellcome.ac.uk http://wellcomeimages.org
109	Fig. 34. Junction of Friary Street and Abbey Street, Nuneaton showing approximate locations of Polly Button's house and John Danks's house. Photograph © Steve Moore.
109	Fig. 35. 1888 OS map of Nuneaton, showing location of Astley's hovel, then called Polly Button's Barn. Reproduced from the 1888 Ordnance Survey map.
110	Fig. 36. Illustration showing the location of the Red Lion public house, Wash Lane, Nuneaton c.1885 (image courtesy of John Burton) and the present-day location where the building would have stood (photograph © Alison James).
110	Fig. 37. The location where The Britannia public house stood in 1832 in Abbey Street, Nuneaton. Photograph © Alison James.
111	Fig. 38. Key elements of the map used at Danks's trial overlaid onto the present-day layout of Nuneaton. © SCG Cartography and Design.

INDEX

Page numbers in **bold** refer to figures and those in *italic* denote tables.